IN, BUT NOT OF

OTHER BOOKS BY HUGH HEWITT

FIRST PRINCIPLES (1987)

SEARCHING FOR GOD IN AMERICA (1996)

THE EMBARRASSED BELIEVER (1998)

IN, BUT NOT OF

A GUIDE TO

CHRISTIAN AMBITION

AND THE

DESIRE TO INFLUENCE

THE WORLD

HUGH HEWITT

THOMAS NELSON PUBLISHERS®
Nashville

A Division of Thomas Nelson, Inc.
www.ThomasNelson.com

For Ron Karrenbauer and all extraordinary teachers,
and
for the staff and volunteers of Young Life,
an organization dedicated to all young people.
Learn about it at www.younglife.org. Support it.

Published in Nashville, Tennessee, by Thomas Nelson, Inc.

Published in association with Yates & Yates, LLP,
Attorneys and Counselors, Orange, California.

Scripture quotations are from THE NEW KING JAMES VERSION.
Copyright © 1979, 1980, 1982, Thomas Nelson, Inc., Publishers.

Library of Congress Cataloging-in-Publication Data

Hewitt, Hugh, 1956-
    In, but not of : a guide to Christian ambition and the desire to
influence the world / Hugh Hewitt.
        p. cm.
    ISBN 0-7852-6395-0 (hardcover)
    1. Success—Religious aspects—Christianity. I. Title.
BV4598.3.H48 2003
248.4—dc21   2002155522

Printed in the United States of America
03 04 05 06 07 BVG 5 4 3

Contents

PREFACE

IF IT IS TRUE, AS JESUS SAID IT IS, THAT HE IS "THE WAY, the truth, and the life. No one comes to the Father except through Me" (John 14:6), then salvation—happiness for infinity—depends upon the ability of individuals to hear the gospel.

The effective and mass communication of the gospel depends upon the freedom to proclaim it. Though it is possible to proclaim the gospel in the face of persecution, the unfettered freedom to do so is much, much to be preferred. There are billions of souls who are up for eternal grabs, so the unfettered ability to reach them with the good news is a great and wonderful thing, hard to create and difficult to defend.

The creation and defense of religious liberty requires men and women with power and influence in the world. Such leaders helped found the colonies in America, fight for independence, and secure religious liberty via the First Amendment. Christians today are indebted to the founding generation of this country and to their successors who have made the defense of religious liberty a priority for the more than two hundred years that have followed the ratification of the Bill of Rights.

If you want a history of the Framers' commitment to religious freedom, consult Michael Novak's *On Two Wings: Humble Faith and Common Sense at the American Founding* or David Barton's *Original Intent: The Courts, the Constitution, and Religion.* If you want a vivid picture of the life of the faithful outside an environment in which religious liberty is protected, consult www.opendoorsusa.org. My assumption is, however, that Christian readers will agree that evangelization is a *duty* of all Christians and that religious liberty assists in evangelization.

But do you agree on the need for Christians to pursue power and influence?

Many, many Christians do not. They fear the corrupting effects of power on belief, and the temptations that authority brings with it. These effects are dire when they surface, and these temptations are real. It is much easier to avoid the sins of anger and pride, for example, if you reject the idea and pursuit of worldly power.

Power is dangerous to the soul. A fourteenth-century monk, Thomas à Kempis, warned his readers in the classic *The Imitation of Christ* to fly from the courts of kings and princes.

Those courts were places that traded in intrigue and lies, in violence and betrayal. It took a real saint, like Thomas More, to survive for even a time in such a place. Thomas eventually was forced to choose between service to the church or service to the king, and was beheaded when he opposed Henry VIII.

Positions of power in liberal democracies do not require as much grace as did the English court of Henry. But they do require some grace, and obtaining these positions does require much ambition. In a liberal democracy, power, authority, and influence go *only* to those who seek them.

My view is that Christians of appropriate ability should seek these positions and should use them to protect and extend religious liberty. That also means protecting America from its enemies and extending the influence of Western democracy around the globe, for no amount of religious liberty in America will assist in evangelizing closed and dictatorial societies around the world. Here the extension of American influence is also the extension of religious liberty. Some critics of America ignore this or label it imperialism. But the reality of Western-style religious liberty is not imperial domination or religious absolutism; it is the reality of freedom to hear and freedom to choose. Christians in the third millennium should not ask for more than these freedoms or desire more. Genuine conversion cannot be accomplished by force, and all of recorded human history attests to that.

But they must demand the right to speak their piece in peace and to worship as they see fit. These demands are best met with the assistance of believers of power and influence. This book is for Christians resolved to seek power, authority, and influence. Some of it restates obvious truths, and some sets out fairly complex additional tasks. But without preparation, there is no success, and without success, there will be no influence.

With power, authority, and influence come responsibilities, however, and a host of temptations. Seeking the former without succumbing to the latter is hard to achieve initially, much less to maintain over time. It is my hope that this book will be of some help in both tasks.

PART I

THE CRISIS AND THE CALL

HISTORY HAS KNOWN PERIODS OF GREATER AND LESSER human energy, and those periods of greater energy have been periods when ambition was a passion in good standing. In *The Century of Louis XIV*, Voltaire remarks on the four most admired historical epochs: Periclean Athens, Augustan Rome, Italy under the Medicis, and France under Louis XIV. Since Voltaire's day, one might wish to add to the list the United States of America from presidents Washington through Jefferson and England under Queen Victoria. But what all these periods have in common is their lack of equivocal feeling about ambition. Not that ambition in any of these periods failed to produce its usual perversities, from the Athenian Alcibiades to the American Aaron Burr. But whatever its excesses, ambition has at all times been the passion that best releases the energies that make civilization possible . . .

In the Christian view, the pendulum has swung back and forth, from the doctrine that the meek shall inherit the earth to Max Weber's perception (set forth in *The Protestant Ethic and the Spirit of Capitalism*) that, among the Calvinists of the sixteenth and seventeenth centuries, a sign of being among God's elect is success on earth. As a general statement it seems unexceptional to say that Christianity has not necessarily despised ambition, although it has tended to view excessive preoccupation with ambition for worldly things as misguided.

—Joseph Epstein
Ambition

CHAPTER 1

You Have No Idea Where You Are Going, or When the Trip Will Begin

Among men alive at the time I wrote this book, three had done more to shape our world than any others: a Russian, a Pole, and an American.

It is hard to imagine a more unlikely trio, given their early careers.

The Russian took correspondence courses in literature, spent his twenties in the army, his early thirties in a prison camp, and was teaching math when he turned forty.

The Pole is the son of a tailor, who at twenty was working in a stone quarry, was still studying for the priesthood at twenty-five, and only at forty published his dissertation, an appropriately obscure work for an obscure auxiliary bishop in a Warsaw Pact country.

The American was a sports announcer in Des Moines at the age of twenty-five, and by forty his career as an actor had peaked and fallen.

Alexander Solzhenitsyn would use words to strike at the heart of Soviet communism; Karol Wojtyla—later John Paul

II—would inspire the first lasting resistance to the Soviets in one of their vassal states and later encourage freedom throughout the East; and Ronald Reagan would rally the West to face down every intimidation and to call upon the desperate leaders of the last modern empire, the "Evil Empire," Reagan called it, to "tear down this wall."

Even as late as 1988 it seemed impossible that the Soviets would simply dissolve their empire and walk away from seven decades of ideologically fueled expansion. Even then the KGB and the Red Army seemed impossibly strong. No one realistically believed that the USSR could be defeated.

"Yes, yes, of course," wrote Solzhenitsyn, "we all know you cannot poke a stick through the walls of a concrete tower, but here's something to think about: what if the walls are only a painted backdrop?" He wrote those words in 1975, a decade and a half before the painted backdrop would be pierced. Solzhenitsyn was never a short-term thinker.

None of these three giants was a quick-fix schemer. Each was patient and purposeful, and each followed his ambitions as those ambitions developed. They could not have known their paths, so unlikely did those paths turn out to be. But neither did they rule out anything for themselves at any step of the way—even when scrambling among rocks in a stone quarry, shuffling in prison camp food lines in the Siberian winter or battling near fatal throat cancer, or idling away years behind microphones or awaiting the scripts that stopped coming.

And you should not dismiss what your future might hold, for you have no idea where you are going. This is a book about Christian ambition—about the desire to help shape the world in large ways, and to do so in conformance to Christ's teaching. Your circumstances today may or may not be particularly promising, but circumstances change, sometimes slowly and sometimes in the space of a day.

This generation and the next may not be blessed with giants, and even if they are, they will need—absolutely, positively need—hundreds of thousands of leaders of character, purpose, and ability. Even if you have not shown such traits to date, and even if you have spent half a lifetime discouraged by the flow of events, there are decades ahead and opportunities stacked up to the sky. The obstacles you face cannot possibly be as formidable as those that confronted these three men.

But rising in the world does take will. A French writer on the subject remarked upon the example of a retired colonel on a farm: "The colonel who retires on a farm in the country would have liked to have become a general; but if I could examine his life, I would find some little thing that he neglected to do, that he did not want to do. I could prove to him that he did not want to become a general." In other words, the colonel did not want to be a general badly enough.

I came across that quote in a book I read in 1980, *Ambition* by Joseph Epstein, one of the country's finest essayists. I have placed that anecdote on the table many, many times in front of many, many successful people. Eventually almost everyone comes around to this point of view. Success in the world is pretty much a function of disciplined effort.

Which, of course, raises the stakes quite high for Christians. Given the condition of the world, and given the stakes that ride on the outcome of individuals' choices, believers do not really have the option of declining to become generals.

Had Solzhenitsyn, John Paul II, or Reagan chosen different paths—easier paths—the Soviet Union might well still be where it was, or its dissolution, as painful as it was, might not have been so relatively quiet for the rest of the world.

The reality for all Christians is the obligation to equip themselves for their greatest impact and to seek every opportunity to increase that impact.

And never to suspect that they are not called or that their time has passed them by.

· CHAPTER 2 ·

THE SPECTRUM OF CHRISTIAN AMBITION

"IF I SEE A MADMAN DRIVING A CAR INTO A GROUP OF innocent bystanders," Dietrich Bonhoeffer explained to his sister, "then I can't, as a Christian, simply wait for the catastrophe and then comfort the wounded and bury the dead. I must try and wrestle the steering wheel out of the hands of the driver."

The German theologian, a pacifist, was attempting to convey why he had joined with others to plot an unsuccessful assassination of Adolf Hitler. The most extreme ambition is to attempt revolution. Bonhoeffer tried and failed and was executed on April 9, 1945, as a result.

At the other end of worldly ambition is Francis of Assisi (1181–1226). Although a young man of wealth and position, Francis went through a religious transformation that saw him renounce all his goods, honors, and privileges in exchange for a life of ruthless poverty and service to the poor. He fashioned his rules for his followers from Christ's command to the rich young man to sell everything and follow Him. His ambition became limited to the conversion of souls. Francis's extraordinary gentleness and humility and his "all embracing sympathy" defined him. "Saintlier than any saint," wrote one biographer, "among sinners he was as one of themselves." Francis's estimate of the world's opinion was embedded in his famous phrase: "What a man is in the sight of God, so much he is and no more."

Between a would-be assassin-theologian and history's standard for self-denial, there are tens of thousands of degrees of involvement with the temporal world.

There was Pope Julius II, the warrior pope, born to be first a soldier in, and then the chief general of, the effort to repair and extend the worldly power of the papacy. Though a builder and benefactor of the arts (including his patronage of the careers of Michelangelo and Raphael), he was a far greater warrior than a churchman or a patron.

Thomas More (1478–1535), a remarkable jurist and adviser to King Henry VIII, also moved easily in the world. His capacity on the law bench was so great that although he inherited a huge backlog of legal disputes, every case before his court was at one point decided:

> When More some time had Chancellor been
> No More suits did remain
> The like will never more be seen
> Till More be there again.

But More lived in the age of Henry, and More paid for his loyalty to the Roman Catholic Church with his head.

William Wilberforce entered Great Britain's Parliament in 1780. He experienced a profound conversion in 1786, and wrote in his diary, "My walk is a public one. My business is in the world, and I must mix in the assemblies of men."

In 1789, Wilberforce launched a campaign against the British slave trade. Eighteen years later, in 1807, he succeeded in outlawing it and then began to campaign against slavery across the globe.

Henrietta Mears was a woman of vast ambition. She took charge of Christian education programs at First Presbyterian Church of Hollywood in 1928, and Sunday school attendance rose from four hundred to four thousand in three years. Hundreds of her students committed themselves to full-time ministry. One of them, Bill Bright, founded Campus Crusade for Christ in 1951, and that organization now spans the globe and is a model for reaching the unchurched. Mears also was the force behind the development of Forest Home, one of the most famous American retreat centers.

In 1938, in Gainesville, Texas, a young youth pastor was pointed by his boss toward unchurched high school students. Jim Rayburn went after those kids, and he institutionalized his approach and method in the organization Young Life, which Rayburn founded in 1941. Some sixty years later, this parachurch group has deeply touched the lives of millions of teenagers across the country and around the world, and its more than 2,500-member staff and 28 properties continue to do so today. (There's a lot of stuff about Young Life in this book. It is the organization I primarily support outside my own church because I am so impressed by its inclusiveness, effectiveness, and commitment to excellence. You can investigate it for yourself at www.younglife.org.)

In 1942, William Cameron Townsend went to Guatemala to sell Bibles to the indigenous people there. He found himself among one tribe that did not speak Spanish and discovered that the Scriptures had never been translated into the tribe's language. So Townsend stayed a decade, learned the language, and translated the Scripture into it. He also founded Wycliffe Bible Translators, and that organization has translated the Bible into more than five hundred different languages that had never before been open to the gospel. Along the way, the Wycliffe organization became one of the great linguistic research institutions in the history of the study of languages. Another fifteen hundred translations are under way today.

There are millions of stories of Christians involved with the world but not conforming their values to the values commonly associated with success. This record of innovation and engagement continues through to this day. Close to me in southern California are three extraordinary pioneers of new methods to spread the old gospel. Chuck Smith founded the Calvary Chapel movement and made perhaps the greatest impact on the Protestant church in America in the past fifty years. One of his students, Greg Laurie, took Chuck's work into the crusade field and launched the Harvest Crusades, to which nearly three million people have been drawn in a little over a decade (www.harvestcrusades.org). And Pastor Rick Warren founded Saddleback Valley Community Church and became a pastor to thousands of pastors as well as tens of thousands of his own congregants (www.pastors.org).

Twenty-five years before the writing of this book, Dr. James Dobson left the faculty of the medical school at the University of Southern California with a mission to help save American families. As 2002 ended, he had a daily audience of more than 200 million in more than one hundred countries, and the organization he founded, Focus on the Family, had become a preeminent teaching, research, and leadership institution in America.

This baker's dozen of thumbnail sketches cannot even begin to tell the record of Christian involvement with the world. From the time Christ ascended to the present, His church has mixed "in the assemblies of men."

There have always been ups and downs in this process, and controversies and debates. Some who have worn the title of "Christian" have embarrassed their fellow believers, and others have cowered at the prospect of taking the gospel into the world. But history's record is a silencer of those who argue that Christians are to live apart from the world.

This roll call of inspirational examples, however, could easily be a eulogy for a tradition rather than an encouragement to even greater urgency to be salt and light in the world. In a very practical way, Christians seem to be losing the ability to penetrate the culture. Some have lost their drive. Still others simply lack the skills. Even as political forces gather to effectively expel people of faith from public life, the abilities of those who would gladly fight for their right to remain in the public square are strikingly diminished. Though a treasure of examples is laid up—the gentleness of Francis, the determination of Bonhoeffer, the warrior spirit of Julius, the learning of More, the persistence of Wilberforce, the vision and energy of Mears, Rayburn, Townsend, and Bright, and the modern capabilities of Smith, Laurie, Warren, and Dobson—the church is running out of talent or steam or both.

For the church is in retreat. And there are some Christians (and many non-Christians) who think that is a good thing. The record of the last one thousand years proves them wrong, but the past is no guarantee of the future. Unless individuals resolve to engage the world and lead it, the record hinted at by these examples will quickly become eclipsed by the reality of the post-Christian world.

Others, especially Chuck Colson, have written at length and with wisdom on the sea of change in our times. My aim is not to prove again what he and others have documented, but to speak practical thoughts to those who would prefer that the trajectory of the church would change.

· CHAPTER 3 ·

THE PRESSURE OF THESE TIMES

THREE DECADES AGO, UNION ORGANIZER SAUL ALINSKY committed to text his methods for bringing about radical change in the book *Rules for Radicals*. You might not have heard of Alinsky, but he towers over other would-be American revolutionaries because he influenced not just the unionization movements of the 1930s, 1940s, and 1950s, but also the civil rights movement and the campus radicals of the anti–Vietnam War era. His legacy is a brass-knuckled treatise on how to attack power and destroy consensus, still used by many groups across the nation and the world.

Alinsky was an atheist. "We're talking about revolution," he proclaimed, "not revelation." Like most but not all of the Left, Alinsky believed in changing the here and now; preparing men for an eternal life with or without God was beyond his interest. That focus on the present with its demand for immediate action and results has been a tactical advantage over Christian values for a half century, and that advantage has been exploited to stunning effect. The dominant cultural

13

elite is presently radically Left, and the political elites are balanced between Left and Center Right. (Christians, of course, are found all across the political spectrum.)

Now the church itself is locked in civil war with elements that seem to have committed Alinsky's methods to memory. Whether the Jesus Seminar or ad hoc caucuses within various mainline denominations, tenured apostates within Catholic universities or headline-grabbing God-and-the-environment lobbies, the Left has continued to assault established Christian hierarchies in the hope, sometimes realized, of capturing control or at least dominant influence.

There is no conspiracy, though it is a frequent tactic of the Left to accuse the Center Right of seeing conspiracy everywhere. *Conspiracy* signifies an organized hierarchy issuing orders and mapping strategy. The Left is instead defined by a set of attitudes that tend toward the same decisions and actions so that, unorganized and decentralized as it genuinely is, it brings about the very same results as though it was a highly structured and organized command-and-control operation.

John Arquilla, a professor at the Naval Postgraduate School and a RAND analyst, has written extensively about the new era of "networks and netwars." Multichannel networks of people operate independently of hierarchy, but because of shared values and common tactics, they can move effectively with devastating consequences for established order.

The new networks are evolving before our eyes.

Some are benign, the knitting circles of the Internet age. Think of a user group devoted to crossword puzzles.

Some are lethal and intent upon the destruction of the West, and with it the religious liberty that has allowed Christianity to flourish for sixteen hundred years. Al-Qaeda is the most sinister of the new networks.

Some are simply political and limited in their scope to dominating the institutions of power in the United States. One example is EMILY's List, an organization that coined its name from the first letters in the old political saying that "early money is like yeast." Over the years EMILY's List has used a fund-raising technique termed *bundling*— the coordination of tens of thousands of modest contributions into huge outpourings of cash—to propel itself into superstar status among interest groups. Unfortunately for Christians, the goals of EMILY's List are completely from the Left.

Some of the new networks are embracing Alinsky's rules, and advancing in influence and authority on a daily basis. The near continual agitation for policies unthinkable thirty years ago—assisted suicide or repeal of age-of-consent laws—has brought the Left significant progress. The culture wars of the 1980s and 1990s were actually a series of routs of traditional morals and religious beliefs from the field.

This is hardly news. Few things have been more reported than the collapse of the Christian consensus in the United States and the rise of the postmodern culture. Nobody needs another "decline of the West" essay or a meditation on the goo of process theology/New Age cliché/trendy nihilism.

Instead, I'd like to win a few rounds. I'd like the church (here and throughout this book meaning all "mere Christians" of the C. S. Lewis sort, regardless of denomination) to get up from the ground, shake off the dust, and get back into the game. A lot of Christian leadership seems intent on arguing over who gets the museum keys and who chooses the color of the wallpaper inside the crypt. Another swath is busy organizing the reception committee for Christ's return. Still others are intent on convincing us that we, in fact, didn't lose anything to begin with.

We no longer have time for the intramural league. The attack upon the West and Christianity became undeniable on 9/11, even though some are overcome by fear and cannot bring themselves to survey the field. Within the United States, elites of the Left refuse to confront the reality of hatred for the West, even as they keep up their assault on traditional Christianity. If the fundamental dynamics of the struggles for power and influence in the United States are not changed, the Left will be the decisive winner within a generation. If the Left does indeed triumph both culturally and politically, it lacks the will and the ideology to oppose the attack on the West from outside the West.

It is that simple. It is that stark.

Of course, the apostles faced a much more daunting task in the first century than American Christians do in the twenty-first. And defeat and even suppression of the West would not dent, limit, or in any way harm the truth of the gospel.

But it would make much, much more difficult the execution of the Great Commission. When, as is recorded at the end of the gospel of Matthew, Jesus instructed His disciples to "go therefore and make disciples of all the nations, baptizing them in the name of the Father and of the Son and of the Holy Spirit, teaching them to observe all things that I have commanded you" (28:19–20), He did not send them into a world protected by the Free Exercise Clause of the United States Constitution. But that clause is the result of centuries of strife and persecution, and a guarantee of the right of Americans to execute the Great Commission.

Put another way, Sudanese Christians—horribly persecuted, often to the point of death or enslavement—cannot be succored by an American church that is empty or irrelevant. Hundreds of millions of Chinese may someday win the right to leave the shadows of their house churches and receive the theological legacy of the West, but that legacy will be worthless if it is corrupted or spent. And the missionary zeal, which once animated Europe and America, is at its lowest ebb today, and will surely vanish in the absence of a vibrant and confident church.

Many believers respond to the world's crises with prayer—which is exactly what all believers should do. Pray for the church. Pray for the culture. Pray for conversion and revival.

Pray especially for your enemies.

Many other believers are busy renewing the church by strengthening a particular church.

Which is not only good but also necessary, and indeed

commanded of believers. Every reader is called to be a part of a local church and to serve within that church.

There is, however, a much wider world within which to act, to serve, and to lead. This is the sphere of political and public affairs. Christians in great numbers have deserted this sphere, and those who remain within it are often incompetent, sometimes fanatical, and usually inconsequential.

That has to change if the culture, the country, and the world are going to change.

"The basic requirement for the understanding of the politics of change is to recognize the world as it is," wrote Alinsky. "We must work with it on its terms if we are to change it to the kind of world we would like it to be. We must first see the world as it is and not as we would like it to be. We must see the world as all political realists have, in terms of 'what men do and not what they ought to do,' as Machiavelli and others have put it."

Christians have a head start on understanding the world as it is, because Christians begin with an understanding that man is fallen and that sin is everywhere and a part of everyone's life. It is familiar territory for believers when they read Alinsky's conclusions:

It is not a world of peace and beauty and dispassionate rationality, but as Henry James once wrote, "Life *is*, in fact, a battle. Evil is insolent and strong; beauty enchanting, but rare; goodness very apt to be weak; folly very apt to be defiant; wickedness to carry the day; imbeciles to be in great places, people of sense in small, and mankind generally unhappy. But the world as it stands is no narrow illusion, no phantasm, no evil dream of the night; we wake up to it forever and ever; and we can neither forget it nor deny it nor dispense with it." Henry James's statement is an affirmation of that of Job: "The life of man upon earth is a warfare."

Even Christians nod their heads as they read Alinsky, James, and Job, though they are generally limited in their response to how the world is. In recent years, Christians in vast numbers have given up on the idea of changing the world, and focused instead on building their congregations, praying for a wide variety of good and godly causes, including missions work.

California Christianity seems especially focused on inviting friends to church, giving some time and money to inner-city poverty relief and mission trips to Mexico. These are all exceptionally good undertakings—make no mistake about that. They should not only continue but also expand in scope and intensity. Changing the circumstances of individual lives is very much an obligation for every believer.

"There are no *ordinary* people," wrote C. S. Lewis. "You have never talked to a mere mortal. Nations, cultures, arts, civilizations—these are mortal, and their life is to ours as the life of a gnat. But it is immortals whom we joke with, work with, marry, snub, and exploit—immortal horrors or everlasting splendors." Given this perspective, that each soul is immortal, changing the trajectory of a soul's path is a matter of infinite consequences. So the tasks and efforts touched on are supremely important.

But then so, too, is the world. If inviting nonbelievers to worship matters, then so does preserving the freedom to worship. If ministering to the needs of the poor is a mandate, then changing the policies creating poverty is very much within that mandate. And if building shelter in developing countries is part and parcel of a Christian's burden, so is the destruction of the power of tyrants who oppress peoples around the globe. Taking first steps on a path is not running an entire race.

Two decades after the Moral Majority and a decade after the Christian Coalition, American Christians have pretty much given up on changing their culture through politics. The marginalization of the Christian Right is profound and deserved in many ways. Its leaders often appeared as bullies, its statements fanatical, and some of its troops wild-eyed.

And, of course, its "victories" were transient, if not totally contrived to begin with. Use any measure: religious liberty, the state of public education, the availability of porn, the abuse of drugs, the prevalence of abortion, the continued splintering of family. These are indices not only of social destruction, but also, inversely, of the impact of Christianity upon its culture. As the obvious tallies of sin rise, one can conclude only that Christianity's impact has fallen.

How to change this?

Not through a renewed Moral Majority or a newer, improved version of the Christian Coalition certainly. Rather, every Christian must consciously commit to impacting the culture. To do that requires influence. Influence is not an automatic gift bestowed on good people. It is earned. It falls to a huge variety of people, most of whom consciously plan on acquiring influence.

Christians need to seek influence. They need to acquire it. They need to use it once they have it. But first they must acquire it.

This is a book about acquiring influence. It is primarily directed at young adults under age forty-five, though it is usable by the middle-aged and even seniors. There is little mystery about what works and what doesn't when it comes to acquiring influence, but some methods are clearly criminal—blackmail, for example—and others ought to be off-limits to Christians.

Though obvious, the means of acquiring influence are infrequently discussed among Christians. Thus what follows is a very "worldly" discussion, and not for the fainthearted who think worldly ambition is itself evil or who are repulsed by Alexander Hamilton's blunt conclusion that "fame is the highest calling of the noblest minds."

But if you have bought this book or received it as a gift, then you or someone you know thinks you have the right stuff to lead in the world, and you or someone you know has decided to add a little provocative writing and some very practical advice to your thought process.

The first few chapters are for young adults—between eighteen and about thirty. Older folks can find some useful stuff there, but advice on academic credentials comes a little late for most people on the far side of thirty. The balance of the book is applicable throughout the five stages of an adult's life.

Your twenties are stage one. Stage two takes you from around thirty to around forty-five—the years of professional apprenticeship and usually small and demanding children. Professionally you will be at your peak abilities from forty-five to sixty, which is stage three. From sixty to the onset of physical disability, stage four, is the time to mentor and transition. And when the body begins to break down, you can relax and reflect.

Influence tends to ebb as the body does, even as its acquisition peaks with professional accomplishment. These rough segments have fuzzy, permeable borders, of course, but they work well as general guideposts. This is a critical point: you will find it difficult to obtain influence in your peak years if you have done nothing about it prior to entering the shadow of fifty. And once you have influence, it is very hard to relinquish it.

Which is why everyone who thinks he wants influence and who believes he wants to lead should think at least a little on the myth of Er, which is described in detail in the next chapter. It may be a little odd to begin a book about Christian leadership with a reference to the closing chapter of Plato's *Republic*, but that's where we find the myth. And it teaches that a decision to seek influence and a decision to lead carry huge implications for your life, not all of them good.

PART II

BEFORE THE CAREER BEGINS

[PATTON'S] REAL FORMAL EDUCATION WAS NOT necessarily through class instruction, where his performance was always mediocre at best, but rather through his own disciplined course of reading . . . In his journal of 1906 he was already making systematic and detailed lists of books to read. And he was planning future acquisitions for his own library that would eventually reach five hundred personally annotated volumes . . . Immediately after graduating from West Point . . . Patton began a lifelong habit of reading constantly, often trying to match his current assignments with germane literary and military masterpieces that might put his own concrete experiences of the moment into a more conceptual context of the ages.

—Victor Davis Hanson
The Soul of Battle

[CHURCHILL] WOULD ALSO BECOME A LIFELONG omnivorous reader of newspapers and one of the most well-informed men in the world on the events of his times. At Sandhurst, as at Brighton, he was scanning column after column of newsprint every evening.

—William Manchester
The Last Lion

CHAPTER 4

STUDY THE MYTH OF ER

IN THE BOOK *THE REPUBLIC*, PLATO HAS SOCRATES TELL his audience the story of Er, "a strong man," who died in a war. On the "tenth day, when the corpses, already decayed, were picked up, he was picked up in a good state of preservation. Having been brought home, he was about to be buried on the twelfth day; as he was lying on the pyre, he came back to life, and, come back to life, he told what he saw in the other world."

What Er saw was very complex, but there was judgment, and then there was a choice by each soul of a new life. The souls were allowed as much time as they wished to search among an abundance of new lives, and they made their choices based upon the knowledge they had accumulated in their just finished lives. The spokesman for the Fates that governed this process warned the arrivals: "Even for the man who comes forward last, if he chooses intelligently and lives earnestly, a life to content him is laid up, not a bad one. Let the one who begins not be careless about his choice. Let not the one who is last be disheartened."

But the first soul did not listen and quickly rushed to choose the life of a powerful tyrant. As he turned to consider all the aspects of the life he chose, "he beat his breast and lamented the choice," because along with the power came horrible crimes, including "eating his own children."

Others chose new lives of great variety. Ajax, the warrior of Troy, chose to become a lion, for instance, while another, the woman Atalanta, "saw the honors of an athletic man and couldn't pass them by."

The last to choose was Odysseus, whom you may know as Ulysses—the famed warrior and voyager. The tale of Odysseus' long voyage home from Troy to Ithaca has captured many hearts, with its encounters with the Cyclops, the Sirens, and various Greek gods. Odysseus eventually reached his home and reclaimed his kingdom and his wife, having lived an adventure that truly has endured all the time since it was written. In *The Republic* we meet this figure again as he chooses the circumstances of his next life:

And by chance Odysseus' soul had drawn the last lot of all and went to choose, from memory of its former labors it had recovered from love of honor; it went around for a long time looking for the life of a private man who minds his own business; and with effort it found one lying somewhere, neglected by the others. It said when it saw this life that it would have done the same even if it had drawn the first lot, and was delighted to choose it.

The Republic ends less than a page after Odysseus makes his choice. Scholar Allan Bloom—you may remember his best-seller *The Closing of the American Mind*—writes about Odysseus that "all he needed was to be cured of love of honor (a form of spiritedness), and he could live the obscure but happy life of Socrates," a quiet life of contemplation and philosophy. Odysseus chose, on his second time around, to stop all the glory and all the war. He wanted peace and quiet.

Every Christian faces the same choice but with full knowledge of how the world is working, stripped of the myths of the ancients, and clearly aware of Christ's place in the world and God's plan for history. Many Christians choose to ignore the world and focus on Scripture and the life of a local congregation. They fear, with good reason, that the world can and does corrupt people; that it can and does turn people away from obedience to God's commands. They make the Christian equivalent of Odysseus' choice.

In fact, more and more Christians are opting out of public life. They are disgusted with the raucousness, crudity, and often emotionally and spiritually upsetting struggles for worldly influence. In truth, they fear the combat and the casualties. And many of them fear falling in love with the glories and triumphs of the world, and losing touch with Christ as a result. Terry Eastland is an old friend of mine who has done very well in the world, having authored many fine books and led many notable publications. Moreover, he has always managed to maintain his reputation for integrity and character even as he has moved among and worked with the most powerful figures over three decades in Washington, D.C.

Terry has been fond of quoting Paul's description of Demas, a disciple of Paul, who left Paul. Demas left, according to Paul, because he "loved this present world" (2 Tim. 4:10). Nothing else is said about Demas, so we are left to wonder what exactly that meant, but theories abound. Demas might have been led away by money, power, position, fame, or all of these plus more.

Odysseus swore off public life when given a free choice informed by his experience, and Paul condemned a too-worldly one-time follower. The myth and the Scripture are warning signs.

It is easier to stay quietly within the confines of the church and busy only with the particulars of church work. It is easier to have limited objectives; easier to wash your hands of the world. But it is not necessarily better, and the choice of a retiring life may simply be cowardice dressed up as prudence.

If you choose to pursue influence, you will do well to learn some things early on.

CHAPTER 5

ASSEMBLE THE RIGHT CREDENTIALS

THESE NEXT FEW CHAPTERS ARE AIMED MORE AT younger people than older ones, and this particular chapter has specific applicability to readers considering their next steps in the credential race. Even though more and more older people are returning to school to add a credential to their résumés, these decisions are largely made by people under the age of twenty-five.

Which is why most of these decisions are badly thought through.

The good news is that most decisions made before the age of thirty are not irreversible. Screwups are best experienced before that age, and false starts hardly matter.

But it is still preferable to get it right the first time. So here are the rules:

1. Status matters. All universities are not created equal, and credentials from prestigious universities matter a great deal more than those acquired from unknown universities. People

who tell you otherwise are being falsely modest or attempting to make you feel better.

2. Because status matters, you can expect it to cost more. Be prepared to spend more on degrees from prestigious universities because they are worth more. The cost hardly matters when you spread it over the years of your professional life. If you are accepted into many schools, always pick the school with the most status. Money should enter into it only if there is a tie—for example, you have been accepted at both Harvard and Yale Law Schools. (Indeed, I think the advantage of a prestigious degree is so great, I believe tuition loans are among the very few debts a young adult ought to incur.)

3. A Bachelor of Arts is not enough. The exceptions to this rule are few and far between, and the absence of a postgraduate degree must still be compensated for via some other extraordinary credential, such as military service or a successful start-up of your own company.

4. The only postgraduate degrees that have stand-alone value are the J.D. (a lawyer), the M.D. (a doctor), and the MBA (a boss). Master's and Ph.D. degrees have value but only if they are properly explained. Sometimes you don't get the chance to explain, and all those years of study end up helping you very little—if at all.

5. The stand-alone postgraduate degrees are worth having even if you never use them. Younger people often discard this advice because they first hear it from the lips of parents, but it is very true. The world is full of lawyers, doctors, and busi-

nessmen who are not practicing the skills they acquired in a formal sense, but whose training deeply changed their approach to life.

6. Never, never, never take yourself out of the running for a credential. "I won't get in" is a guarantee of being shut out. Apply everywhere and get used to rejection. A ding letter won't kill you, but never knocking means never getting in.

7. With a handful of exceptions—Harvard, Yale, and Stanford—do not obtain your graduate degree from the same university as your B.A.

8. Go abroad for at least one semester and preferably for a couple of years. Postgraduate credentials from abroad are enormously valuable in the United States when an American carries them. A note to readers from abroad: American decision makers often unfairly devalue degrees from foreign universities when they are not carried by an American. That's just the way it is. Don't expect much sympathy from U.S. employers.

9. Undergraduate grades matter only so far as they affect your admission to graduate schools. They matter not at all for getting prestigious jobs down the road. In graduate school, class rank matters, as do some corollary marks of excellence (membership on a law review, etc.), but it is 90 percent the degree and the institution. If you miss the opportunity to obtain status credentials as a young adult, you will have to compensate down the road.

10. Treat the hunt for academic credentials as seriously as a hunt for a job because it is the hunt for a job. Obtaining

these credentials smooths the way for ambition at every turn, and their absence impedes your rise in the world. Spend the time necessary to investigate your choices and to prepare your applications. Cut classes and shortchange studying in order to get applications right—this is just a cost-benefit calculation, and one you should be continually making.

11. This rule is crucial. If you are not admitted to an institution that you had identified as one where you wanted to go, do not accept second best. Wait a year and try again. There are many things to do in the interim, including living in a new city or abroad while supporting yourself by flipping burgers. If the credential is worth having, it is worth waiting for.

12. Christian schools can be tremendous sources of inspiration and learning, but some will put you at a significant disadvantage for credentials. Non-Christians and even some Christians are simply not aware of the reputations of such institutions and will assume that they are inferior academically. Unless your faith needs the support (and this is true for many people), do not reflexively rule out secular schools. If you do attend a Christian university as an undergraduate, pursue your graduate degree at a secular university.

These rules will not endear me to people who have followed different paths and who have succeeded in careers and life. They are, however, generally true and generally should be followed by individuals aiming to impact their world. Christians are warned repeatedly and wisely about the sin of pride, and the trumpeting of great credentials would fall under the heading of that sin. But—a crucial *but*—recognizing the value of the credential and then using it in the world is in no way connected to pride and quite obviously connected to purpose.

Recall Paul's point about his credentials and status among the Jews: "Circumcised the eighth day, of the stock of Israel, of the tribe of Benjamin, a Hebrew of the Hebrews; concerning the law, a Pharisee; concerning zeal, persecuting the church; concerning the righteousness which is in the law, blameless" (Phil. 3:5–6). He was citing his credentials in order to establish his authority. Your authority will not depend upon your credentials, but will be buttressed by them. It is that simple.

CHAPTER 6

Learn How You Got Here

You live in what is broadly understood to be the West. If you succeed in acquiring influence, it will almost certainly be over some part, large or small, of the West. The numbers of Westerners who have influenced a portion of the world not in the West are either part of pop culture or individuals of extraordinary talent. Most of us are well served by developing our ambition in light of what the West values. In other words, it is very hard for an American to influence the future of India.

Though *the West* can mean different things to different people, it generally means the countries that have largely embraced the idea of individual liberty for a decent interval of centuries. Sometimes that interval has been interrupted—as in Germany—but for most of the past three hundred years the rules of the West have been those of democracy and the values those of the Enlightenment.

Today the West includes the United States, Canada, Great Britain, most of Europe, Australia, New Zealand, and Israel. It could at one time coherently be referred to as Christendom, though no more. Now the borders of the West are most closely aligned with those where the practices and rules of democratic capitalism are in place and functioning.

Most of the world's population do not live in the West, and your influence upon people in the non-West will be indirect at best. Your likely arena, at its broadest, is limited to the parts of the world that will not reject you as a total stranger. Practically this means the U.S., though a handful may develop some non-Western pop through politics or business.

The West did not just show up on a map following World War II. It is the product not just of geography, but also of individuals and ideas. The West has a history, and you need to know it.

Sure, it is your history. It explains why you are where you are and how you got there. But quite a few happy and good people, many of them wonderful believers as well, function as they ought to without a clue as to how they arrived where they are. Nor are they curious.

The influence of such people on the world is quite limited. If you want to have a share in the conduct of affairs, whether of your business, your city, your culture, or your country, you are going to have to know how we all ended up here, at least in outline, at least in regard to chapter headings. Don't expect the world to take you seriously if you haven't bothered to get the basic story line down.

Almost every successful job applicant will have taken the time to do an investigation before showing up on interview day. In these days of Internet connections and search engines like Google, there is no excuse for arriving at the interview with only a vague understanding of what the company does and who runs the company. If you have a campus interview with Procter and Gamble, and lack an up-to-date grasp of the profitability of the company and the names of the executive team on your lips, expect a pleasant talk but no callback. The same dynamic will hold true for any midcareer professional making a decision to switch jobs or fields, or for any returnee to the workforce. Business expects that the genuinely interested and prospectively productive applicant will have enough curiosity to scout the firm's Web site.

If you expect to influence something bigger than a business—say, a city, a state, or the federal government—then you had better at least do as much background research as you would do for a job interview. With the apparent exceptions of music and movies, the world is not open to seduction by dummies. (I say "apparent" because the folks running these industries should not be understood to be the folks performing on stage or screen.)

"Every nation or group of nations has its own tale to tell," wrote Winston Churchill in 1956, a decade after he had saved the West from Hitler. "Knowledge of the trials and struggles is necessary to all who would comprehend the problems, perils, challenges, and opportunities which confront us today." True then. Truer now.

If you want to accumulate real influence, and not just a tiny bit of it, then you have to know the story of the West. The good news is that the outline is fairly easy to absorb, even if you have not spent a minute on it up until this point. The better news is that the process of getting down the basics will almost certainly addict you to the process, so the outline you absorb will continue to increase in detail and complexity. In very short order, whether you are 18, 30, 46, or 60, you will have filled in the gaps that developed due to the press of other parts of your life.

This is what you need to get down: the Jews, the Greeks, the Romans, the English, and of course, the Americans. You can go about this any way you like, but if you strike out for a formal, textbook learning, things will go badly quickly, and you are likely to give up the effort and with it any real shot at real influence.

Instead I suggest you allow the popularizers of history to work their magic. Because our education in this area is so bankrupt, a new generation of writers has sprung up to fill the deep need that people feel to understand where they and their countries came from. They do not write for academics; they write for you and me. These writers put, as documentarian Ken Burns is fond of saying, "the 'story' back into 'history.'" When Burns did this with his PBS series *The Civil War,* the entire country put down its remote and was captivated. We are a visual culture now, but books can still work their magic. Here is one short course:

The Jews. No doubt you have an advantage here. Most believers have absorbed the general outline of the wanderings and then the ups and downs of God's chosen people. But it's still an incomplete story when only Scripture is relied upon because Scripture does not relate how the history of the Jews affected the vast world around them. In 1998 Thomas Cahill wrote *The Gifts of the Jews: How a Tribe of Desert Nomads Changed the Way Everyone Thinks and Feels.* Start here. The Jews invented the idea of a developing history that could be shaped, though its future could not be known. They were given tasks by God to complete, and this gave structure to their civilization in a unique way. Abraham was charged "to be a blessing," and the ethics of the West began to take shape.

The Greeks. The idea of freedom was born in Greece, as were many ideas on how best to preserve and defend it. Ideals of behavior also developed here, some parallel with those given the Jews by God, some radically different. "The birthplace of civilization" is the generally accepted title for ancient Greece. But it is a hard place to understand, even in passing. For both Greece and Rome I suggest backing into your outline of history through readable fiction. Enough of the story is there to get you on your way.

You are lucky to live after Steven Pressfield has written *The Gates of Fire* and *Tides of War.* The first book tells the story of the Spartans' heroism at the battle of Thermopylae. The second exhausts but thrills the reader with an account of the Peloponnesian War—the twenty-seven-year civil war between Sparta and Athens. In a different age you would have already read Thucydides' *A History of the Peloponnesian War.* You probably haven't, and you likely lack the patience to do so now. This pair of novels will do.

The Romans. Here again you have been cheated, even those

of you who finished your schooling before the widespread collapse of public education. You ought to have read Plutarch. You probably haven't. Your glimpse of the glory of Rome is from the movies, and great as *Gladiator* was, it was nothing compared to Rome.

Again you are lucky. Another novelist of power decided to renew Rome's hold on the imagination of the curious. Colleen McCullough began a series of six novels with *The First Man in Rome,* which follows the career of Gaius Marius, who served seven times as the leader of Rome and was among its greatest generals.

Marius gained the highest office in 107 B.C. Julius Caesar was assassinated on March 15, 44 B.C. McCullough's series spans those sixty years, but with enough detail and insight to give you a handhold on the centuries through which Rome rose and fell. You don't have to know the dates of the three Punic Wars, and you don't have to read Gibbons's *Decline and Fall of the Roman Empire* to "get" Rome. But you do have to get it. Somehow. I suggest you start with McCullough.

The English. The first line in the first chapter of Winston Churchill's *A History of the English Speaking Peoples* reads: "In the summer of the Roman year 699, now described as the year 55 before the birth of Christ, the Proconsul of Gaul, Gaius Julius Caesar, turned his gaze on Britain." Four volumes later—four of the most wonderful, engaging, rollicking volumes on any bookshelf anywhere—the reader is on the threshold of World War I. You need to read these volumes.

I urge my law students to do this every year. They will never understand the Constitution, I tell them, unless they know the story of Great Britain. Some believe me and read the books. They are inevitably the class stars. Most of them enjoy the read, even though they are pressed for time as only law students can be. But even if history is not for you, this is the outline you must have.

The Americans. Churchill's volumes take you to the eve of the Great War, and along the way provide a brief but thorough summary of the founding of the American colonies, their war against Great Britain, and the history of our country throughout the 1800s. His chapters on the Civil War give an overview that ought to be put into the hands of every junior high student in order to avoid the embarrassment that comes whenever we survey the next generation's collective grip on history.

But the "American century" is the twentieth century, and Churchill does not deal with it. A different English historian does—Paul Johnson in *Modern Times,* one of the most influential books of the last quarter century. Read it, and American politics as well as the struggles against fascism and communism may finally make sense to you.

That's the short course on how we got here. Fourteen volumes may seem like a lot, but they are not. In fact, that number should be a small portion of the reading you routinely do over the course of a year. (If the prospect of reading—a lot— daunts you, then you are not serious about genuine influence. The people who run the world are readers and constantly in search of more information.)

Understanding the outline of the history of the West is vital because it will allow you to make sense of the debates of today and tomorrow. It is an admission ticket to the debate.

Almost every serious person I have met in the twenty-five years that I have been at work in the world has had this outline down. He knew the stories of the Jews, the Greeks, the Romans, the Brits, and our own history. Not that there was a quiz. There never is *a* quiz. The quiz is always under way, and the inspection is ongoing.

The people who run businesses, governments, organizations—the world, in fact—are continually on the lookout for talent. Some talent can be specific, computer programming, for example, or Spanish translation. But leadership is always looking for the next generation of leadership, and that is not a specific talent. It is a package of skills and disciplines, one of which is intellectual curiosity. This curiosity is the first ingredient of leadership.

How do leaders recognize this curiosity in the next generation? If job seekers haven't been curious enough to figure out how we came to be here and why we have become the people we are, it is hardly likely that their curiosity is other than a personal sort. Harsh, but true. Next candidate please.

There are 280 million Americans. They are your fellow citizens, and they are also your competition. If only 1 percent of them have the outline down, then there are millions of people struggling for influence over the world who possess the advantage of knowing the basics. Give yourself a shot at competing with them.

Christians especially need this outline because they will often be called upon to defend the worldview that God initiated history, that He has a plan for it, that Christ entered history at a time and a place with a specific purpose, and that history is moving toward a conclusion. Even if ambition to lead and to rise has no part in your makeup whatsoever, how are you going to fulfill the Great Commission if you haven't got a clue about what's been happening in the world in the two thousand years since Jesus entered it?

Sure, it's a lot of reading, but it is the sort of reading that you will enjoy. Just do it. The road goes on and on once you acquire the taste, and other reading lists are embedded in this book, but your own path will show itself.

Now a caution. The world is full of terrible books, both those that are time wasters and those that are deeply, horribly wrong about the way the world works and how it came to be this way. The first sort are mistakes, but the latter can be deadly. Which is why there is no such thing as an innocent suggestion of a book to read.

Younger adults have to be careful in their selection. Most college students can survive a lousy professor in the sciences or a boring professor in humanities or politics. Charismatic professors on a mission—they're dangerous. Marx and Hitler launched their massacres of millions with books, books that purported to give an outline of history. Millions read these books and believed them. They have their modern counterparts. So it is best to get your suggestions from reliable individuals—individuals whose character impresses you as much as their intellect.

CHAPTER 7

RECOGNIZE THAT THE CHOICES AND HABITS OF YOUR SCHOOL YEARS WILL BECOME THOSE OF YOUR LIFE

IT HAS BEEN A QUARTER CENTURY SINCE I LEFT COLLEGE and twenty years since I graduated from law school. But I have been teaching law students for nearly a decade and I frequently lecture on college campuses, so I can say with authority that not much has changed. Young adults waste vast, vast amounts of time. This appears to be part of the software built into the body of a twenty-something, but just because the habits of insouciance (look it up or wear it as a label) are widespread doesn't mean they should go unexamined.

I am not a scold or a puritan. Don't worry that the next few pages will be full of warnings about the dangers of drinking beer, dancing, and keeping late-night hours. Aristotle's advice about aiming for moderation in everything serves well at this age to cover all pastimes, and the older readers are much more at risk from excess than the younger ones. Later chapters will address how many a treasure of carefully accumulated influence is lost because of too many drinks or a single mistake with the opposite sex. Although Christ's standards for conduct are the same regardless of age, the world is much more forgiving of youthful indiscretions than of middle-aged ones.

An example: as a young lawyer in the White House during the Reagan presidency, I had the job of reading FBI background investigation reports on nominees to various federal jobs. Occasionally the bureau's interviews with old acquaintances, friends, and neighbors would turn up a tale or two from a job seeker's school years, but I don't recall that these escapades ever mattered. Adult screwups, however, closed the door on many applicants. There is a fine judge, for example, Douglas Ginsburg, who would today be on the United States Supreme Court but for the fact that he smoked dope at a party as an adult and his opponents inflated the episode into a hanging offense. The same incident had not come up during his original confirmation as a judge, but when his name was advanced for the high court, this smoke became the torpedo that sank his nomination.

I can assure you that thousands of federal officeholders did much worse than smoke marijuana while in school, yet a general amnesty—unspoken but real—has existed for years over all but the most serious screwups during the school years.

Having said that, I advise you to avoid the extremes of school life that seem to dominate the headlines and the cable shows these days. The excesses of spring break have now spawned a series of videos and television specials that document a sad sort of frenzy among young people. Sexual excess can often scar people during these years as well, but the rise of casual coupling is well documented, though its effects are not. And even at Christian colleges the widespread prevalence of porn is in marked contrast to the campuses of a couple of decades ago. There would have been shame associated with trips by undergrads to the adult bookstore in the seedy part of town, but there does not appear to be much shame associated with Internet porn surfing. Again, these habits are hard to break and will certainly diminish your soul, even if the world does not know about them or, knowing, does not care. Many adults whose lives are disabled by various addictions—to alcohol, drugs, porn, etc.—took the first steps on these horrific roads while they were undergraduates. They will not rise in the world, at least for long, if they do not reverse those habits.

Coaches can be sages, and they learn to package their wisdom in short bursts that can be transferred to athletes quickly and at pretty high volumes. One of my friends is Coach Jerry, for years a very successful high school basketball coach. Coach Jerry hails from Rhode Island originally, so he cannot pronounce the *H* in Hugh. This scrambles his advice to me sometimes, but my favorite nugget from Coach Jerry is this: "You see," he says, "life is a habit. Remember that. Life is a habit."

He's right, of course. Most of what we do every day is what we did the day before or the week before or the month before. Occasionally major breaks arrive to force a realignment of our habits, such as leaving for college or grad school, starting a new job, getting married, or having a child, but even then we carry forward as many habits as we can into the new circumstances.

Conduct an inventory of your life, and look for the patterns from the number of cups of coffee you have in the morning to the route you drive to work to the times and manner in which you get exercise. Habits. All of them.

The school years are critical because they are molds for the habits you develop concerning mind work. The patterns you fall into regarding what and how you choose to learn will replicate and replicate. It is highly unlikely that a lazy, unfocused undergrad will morph into a disciplined, diligent law school or business school student, or that a grad student of any type who takes extra years to complete degrees or who treats his teaching duties with disdain will become an efficient and trustworthy professional upon the conferral of a terminal degree.

Change can happen. It is possible. But it is easier to set up productive habits and fall into them than to indulge destructive ones that must be broken later.

So here are some suggestions for the young adult with the student years still ahead:

Choose teachers, not courses. Of course, you have to satisfy requirements, and you will inevitably have to suffer through some terrible professors. But the only academic lessons that will last for you will be those driven home by the talent of an exceptional teacher.

Great teachers are usually tough teachers, but better a C from a great teacher than an A from a time-serving dummy. You will not believe that last line because of the press to advance to the next level, a progress that depends in part upon your grade point. The good news is that your GPA is much less significant than your graduate admission test scores, and grade inflation is making the C an endangered species.

But even if it were true that the C would hobble you, and four C's would hobble your advancement greatly, you would be better off to have sat through brilliant lectures than to have taken "Rocks for Jocks" (as we referred to Harvard's intro geology class in the '70s) or some such garden path course. One of the first four courses I took as a college student was urged on me by an adviser, and the professor—whose name I cannot recall—led me through the world's great autobiographies and introduced me to Augustine, among others. This man had a reputation for tough grading, but I had been convinced that did not matter at all, and that was wonderful advice.

Avoid courses where the reading list is dominated by titles published within the past three decades. Any author or idea worth reading or learning will have staying power. The vast majority of authors and ideas do not have staying power. So if you spend a lot of time reading authors and ideas that have appeared only recently, you will be wasting a great deal of your time. Skip those authors and those ideas. If they turn out to have staying power, you can read them at your leisure in middle age.

This advice, if followed, simplifies your course and major selection dramatically. Skip over the gender studies and the peace studies junk, and go directly to fields of studies that were fields of studies a half century ago. At least you can be assured that employers will not laugh when they see your field of concentration on a résumé. (I would never consider hiring a graduate from a department of gender studies. Though there might be some insight in that course of study, most of it is nonsense, and PC nonsense at that.)

Within a traditional major, look for courses with reading lists weighted toward traditional titles. There is a reason why they are called great books. The "resale" value of these courses is high, which means that employers and other key people will recognize that you hold quality and tradition in high esteem—an important thing.

Carefully consider extracurricular pursuits. They are valuable only if they have value beyond the university. All of these pursuits absorb time. In exchange for that time you should be getting either friends or skills. The best of these should provide both.

Most of your success in the world will depend upon your friends and your employers. The university is where you will form habits in the acquisition of friendships, many of which will last a lifetime. Choose pastimes that will bring you into the circle most likely to introduce you to friends of the sort worth having.

A few of these pursuits can give you some skills. If your campus has a decent daily newspaper, join it and work hard within its ranks. The talents necessary to the production of a daily newspaper are real skills with real value. Most colleges no longer bother to teach students how to write, much less edit or report. Even the techniques of physical production have value in a hundred different settings.

And, truth be told, the most curious minds are drawn to these papers. Some campus papers are full of political bilge, but that can be discounted. The intensity of journalism—not the classroom sort, but the business of getting out a daily— seems to carve discipline into students.

Political clubs are next to worthless, a lesson I learned too late to save me a lot of wasted time. Inevitably silly scrambles for titles and control of the Xerox machine creep into all such organizations. If you are drawn to politics, skip the semi-pros and the minors, and go directly to the bigs. There will always be a campaign for a real office run by a real candidate in need of real volunteers. Expend your energy there, and learn something.

Intramural sports are fun. And that's all they are. Moderation in everything.

Intercollegiate athletics represent the high-water mark for most athletes, and thus the plateau of their achievement. It is not a high plateau, and unless it is a means of paying for the education, I doubt whether this investment of time is worth the opportunities it costs.

The list goes on and on, but the calculation should be obvious: a choice to do A is also a choice not to do B. Time is finite, though it doesn't seem so to many university students.

CHAPTER 8

MASTER AT LEAST ONE AREA OF PASSING INTEREST TO POWERFUL PEOPLE

PEOPLE RISE IN THE WORLD BECAUSE THEY ATTRACT the attention and approval of powerful people. Talent attracts some of that attention, but talent is not always sufficient to hold that attention or earn approval. Talent can get you a foothold in an organization, but not advancement.

The most powerful component of advancement is mutuality of interest with people who control advancement. That's a big phrase—"mutuality of interest." It means liking the same things that bosses or superiors like. Generally this "mutuality of interest" allows for friendships to develop and grow. Typically, though, friendship—genuine friendship of the sort I write about later—cannot exist between two people more than a handful of years apart in age because that age gap prohibits genuine mutuality of interest.

For the same reason you cannot hope, nor should you want, to be friends with the people who can advance you in the world. Still, if you have something to offer him or her beyond talent, then the possibility of patronage exists.

A crass but true example is golf. It is a running joke around law schools that young lawyers must master the basics of the game—it's what the senior partners play. And golf can advance many business relationships as well as nurture friendships. It is a five-hour conversation punctuated by, in my instance, one hundred plus swings of a club. You can get a lot of talking done in five hours.

And I can't tell you how many times I have heard significant people say they learn more about an individual from a round of golf than from ten business meetings. This cliché, like many others, contains truth. A round of golf allows close inspection of integrity. Did a player cheat? Of poise. Did he blow up? Of humor. Was the conversation witty and self-deprecating? Of general likability. Not a bad return for an investment of a few hours.

So a familiarity with golf is a good thing. But you won't be able to golf with most of the people who will advance or hinder your place in the world. You will need something else beyond that particular talent and beyond a nice set of skills as well.

The best thing to have is depth of intellect, unburdened by pride. That is the beginning of wisdom, and every leader you would want to work for and learn from values wisdom.

But how do you obtain and display depth of intellect?

Well, you can't. All you can do is demonstrate that you'd like to develop it. The outline of the history of the West will not do it for you. Knowing that outline is ambition's safety net, not its trampoline.

What you really need is a pretty in-depth knowledge—a talking and teaching knowledge—of at least one and preferably a few areas of at least passing interest to many people at a level of learning and sophistication who might be in a position to advance or hinder your rise.

Imagine a dinner party with eight people, four of whom are comers and four of whom have already arrived. Imagine as well that the rule of this party is that each of the eight will have to deliver a five-minute talk on an area of interest to him or her and to the group.

Those who have arrived go first. Mr. A holds forth on Bosnia. Mrs. B details her speculations about the latest pictures from the Hubble telescope. Mr. C expands on the conservation efforts of fly fishermen. Ms. D talks at length—she is passionate—about a new book on the slums of late Victorian England.

Now the comers are up to bat. Mr. E leads off with a five-minute discussion of Dickens—he had intended a different subject, but Ms. D's talk of the slums of London in the 1880s reminds him of his passion for Dickens who, though he wrote in an earlier age, saw the coming of the problems described by D and warned of their peril. Ms. F chooses to lighten the mood and talk about the perils of cross-country bike trips. Ms. G has been following the oil industry in Azerbaijan and thinks there are parallels to the Bosnian meltdown and the growing discord there.

Now it's your turn. Do you want to talk about golf?

Mutuality of interest has been established, by the way, between D and E, C and F, and A and G. You would be well served to know something about astronomy, but you don't. You can discuss your out-of-bounds at 16.

The setting of a dinner party is a bit contrived—they do occur, and the conversations do flow from guest to guest, though the formalities are not so strictly observed—but the dynamic of establishing your intellectual credentials is not at all contrived. This is how it works.

Your obvious need is to go deep into at least one area of material that will be of interest to many, if not all, people of accomplishment.

One of my great and good friends—one of my seven roommates in college—can talk your head off about the conspiracy to kill Lincoln, about the Beatles, and about nuclear proliferation. He served nearly a decade on the National Security Council counting nukes and helping to plan how best to halt their spread. He has traveled the world with presidents, and he has argued with some bad actors. At dinner, though, you are much more likely to hear about George Harrison's contribution to the Beatles' early years in Hamburg than you are about the climate at the DMZ between North and South Korea.

Now imagine that two candidates for a junior staff job appear for interviews in front of Dan. Both can count nukes. Both have written papers on counting nukes. Both have glowing recommendations from other nuke counters whom Dan knows and admires. But Ms. A couldn't disagree more with Dan about George. George was a slacker, she argues, who could barely play. John carried him night after night, she says. And she points to the opinion of respected rock critic T.

Mr. B doesn't care much for music. "Oh," says Dan, "what are your hobbies?" "I count nukes," replies B.

Who wins?

My point is not that A gets the job because she shares a passion for the same music, but that B forfeits the game by having nothing else. Had he countered with his love of Oxford and his leadership of an American grads club, he'd have sparked Dan's interest because Dan loves Oxford as well. There is no recipe. There are only ingredients.

Which ingredients are you bringing with you to this contest? Golf is nice, perhaps in some instances necessary, but never sufficient. So is an understanding of at least one professional sport; small talk matters. But one-dimensional is just that, and it cannot possibly convey the capacity for intellectual depth.

Don't mistake this as an admonishment to get a hobby. It is advice to identify and go deep into a few areas of interest so that when the spotlight falls on you, you will be prepared to hold it if only for a short time, and to so hold it that your audience—whether one, two, seven, or twenty—concludes, "Hmmm. Sharp stuff."

CHAPTER 9

TATTOOS: DON'T

THIS PIECE OF ADVICE MAY ARRIVE A BIT LATE FOR YOU, but I'd rather discomfit you than leave unsaid a reality check for younger friends.

Fads fade; tattoos don't. These permanent displays of youthful exuberance trigger at best mild amusement, but in some a serious concern about your maturity.

Whether or not you believe that concern to be fair, it is real. The tattoo you covet today will be an obstacle in some situations the rest of your life. Do you need it that much? Is it worth compromising your effectiveness?

This rule of tattoos is easily applied to many other areas of your style of living. Do you do anything to call attention to yourself or to make a statement? If so, is the attention worth it? Most such indulgences are self-defeating, whether it is idiosyncratic hair or clothes, a loud motorcycle, or—later in life—a palatial residence far beyond any ordinary need. The attention you are drawing to yourself is defeating your ambition by marking you as concerned with silly things.

Serious people do not seek attention except for serious purposes.

CHAPTER 10

A MESSAGE ABOUT
VISA/MASTERCARD: DON'T

MOST PIECES OF ADVICE COME WRAPPED IN AT LEAST A little ambiguity. The ambiguity allows the reader to customize the suggestions to his own life. But sometimes it is blunt. This is blunt: don't ever put more on your credit card than you can *easily* pay that very month. Ever. Period. And if you don't have a full-time job, never use it. Period.

Some of you will carry a credit card for the purpose of coping with an emergency. Fine. I am still waiting to hear the story of a university student who *had* to use the plastic to get out of a jam. But it is possible, and having an emergency backup is perhaps wise.

But I do know scores of students who have rung up serious balances on these accounts, balances that begin a lifetime habit of scrambling to fill this hole.

Don't dig this hole. Really. Please.

Everyone knows this. Whether it is 14 percent or 22 percent, the interest charges on these balances are simply thieves living in your life. Because it works so quietly, you hardly notice, and there is nothing like a university student when it comes to ignoring bad news. Many of you think you will pay it off when you get that first job, only to discover that the costs of that first job are pretty high, in rent, transportation, and wardrobe. Monthly obligations go up in those years. Not down. That's also when the student loans start coming due. And if a baby arrives in the first ten years after a diploma, forget about digging out.

Don't go there.

It is possible to rise in the world carrying a burden of debt, but not easy. Only huge talent can pull it off because huge talent can mean enormous productivity. Churchill, for instance, was plagued by debt, as was Disraeli. You cannot live like Churchill or Disraeli because the world will no longer allow such figures to emerge or to skate.

In fact, no one gets to skate on debt anymore. People want to be paid. They come after the deadbeat. Your unpaid bills are referred to collection agencies, which pursue you, and your credit rating is damaged. Once you earn the label of deadbeat, it sticks.

This is a book free of most investment and financial advice. Such matters concern me only as they connect to your ability to get a handhold on the world and climb its various ladders. Debt is grease on the rung above and below you. It will cling to you wherever you go and compromise most of your moves.

Your attitude toward debt is formed as a student. The big credit card companies will make it very easy for you to join the ranks of the indebted. Just say no.

If you have already screwed up and are caught, come clean

to the most responsible person you know, a parent, if that is possible. Don't expect a handout, but try to get financial advice on cleaning up the wreckage. A few thousand dollars can look like a mountain of debt, but it can be cleared away with a bit of discipline.

If you are not now in the hole, think about the pleasure of never having to sit down with another party to get that kind of advice. Think about never having to take a second job just to pay for the excess of a few years ago. Think about never having to declare bankruptcy—a scarlet mark that follows you for years.

This is simple advice that is hard to keep in mind when it is your turn to buy or there is a spring break trip to the islands that you have no cash for. It is much, much better to skip what you cannot afford than to use other people's money now and pay those people later—again and again and again.

PART III

THERE IS NO 9 TO 5—YOUR LIFE FROM 8 A.M. TO 7 P.M.

SWIMMING FOR HIS LIFE, A MAN DOES NOT SEE MUCH of the country through which the river winds, and I probably know little of these years through which I busily work and live, beyond this, how sin and frailty deface them, and how mercy crown them.

—William Gladstone

JOHN ARBUTHNOT FISHER, ENGLAND'S GREATEST admiral since Nelson . . . owed nothing to family, wealth, or social position and everything to merit, force of character and sheer persistence. "I entered the Navy penniless, friendless and forlorn," he told everyone who would listen, including the King. "I have had to fight like hell and fighting like hell has made me what I am." He brought to the fight an exceptional inventory of qualities: Herculean energy, burning ambition, towering ego and self-confidence, and fervent patriotism. He was bold, quick-witted and original, and in everything he did he was passionately involved: for or against, yea or nay.

—Robert K. Massie
Dreadnought

· CHAPTER II ·

Either a Player or a Pastor Be—
But You Can't Be Both

If you are a pastor who has picked up this book because you have had it with the drift of your city, your state, or indeed the entire country, please, put it down.

If you are a seminarian who wants to plan a ministry career that will intertwine with politics, as Jerry Falwell or Pat Robertson has done, please, put it down.

If you are an undergraduate at Westmont or Wheaton or Gordon Cromwell and you have always felt called to pastor in one way, shape, or form, don't let this book turn your head.

Influence in the world is difficult to obtain and requires skills and disciplines that are not at all like those I have observed in the great leaders of the church. It is true that a very few pastors have on a very few occasions served the church and the world at the same time. Augustine, Thomas More, and Thomas Becket, as well as the pastors of revolutionary America, are examples of such unique individuals.

Generally you can choose to rise within the world of the church or within the world of the world. But not both. It will confuse you. It will confuse the faithful. And it will be singularly ineffective in influencing the world.

The most spectacular failure at playing both ways is Reverend Jerry Falwell. I and most other evangelicals I know cringe when we see him appear on any of the many television shows that gladly book him as a spokesman for the evangelical community. I cringe for two reasons.

First, although he is self-evidently a kind and good-humored man, he doesn't seem to understand the American public even a little beyond his corner of it. The American public's views and its sensibilities are very diverse, but there is a consensus on a majority of subjects and an overarching consensus on how to debate issues. Part of this consensus is that preachers are disqualified from participating in discussions of public policy and politics.

Now you may not like that. You may deeply resent it, in fact. You can even successfully argue that it was not always so, and that it is only a relatively recent development in the life of the republic.

But it is undeniably true today. A preacher has next to zero credibility on any issue of politics or public policy outside his own congregation.

There are a host of reasons why this happened, and lots of books are available if you want to read about the decline and fall of preachers' influence. My guess is that the primary culprit is the perceived anti-intellectualism of many pastors on matters of public policy. I say "perceived" because a preacher's logic is not anti-intellectual when it depends on Scripture, but it is undeniably perceived as being so when Scripture is cited.

An example: if in the middle of a debate on capital punishment, an apostle of the Church of Jesus Christ of Latter-day Saints offered as an argument in defense of the death penalty that some passage in the Book of Mormon sanctioned the use of the death penalty, how would you react?

Well, that is the way that almost all non-Christians react to Scripture-based arguments aimed at persuasion. It is the way quite a few Christians react to Scripture-based arguments aimed at persuasion as well.

When Reverend Falwell appears on the little screen, a giant switch in the public's head is clicked off automatically. People may not turn the channel, but the input switch is off. Reverend Falwell can be quite entertaining in the way Geraldo Rivera is quite entertaining, even to those who cannot stand his politics, so the public may watch. But it will not listen.

Reverend Falwell has zero chance of moving public opinion or of influencing the undecided. Nor would any leader of business or academia or government pay other than lip service to his opinions. Reverend Falwell put himself in the penalty box of American politics and public policy a long time ago. He'll never get out.

And pastors who enter public debates will quickly find themselves in the same box, whether they enter from the Right or the Left.

Two decades ago the American bishops of the Roman

Catholic Church entered a phase where they felt compelled to issue edict after edict on such themes as nuclear proliferation and economic policy. The bishops did almost nothing to advance their stated views—in fact, they probably set them back, so great was their collective reputation for fuzzy thinking. And they hurt the Catholic Church directly by offending its adherents who knew better, and indirectly by diverting attention and resources from issues that ought to have concerned them but did not, as recent exposures of sex scandals have painfully revealed.

The Protestant Left is as unskilled as all comers in this regard, particularly on the issue of the environment. I can recall with horror hearing a minister proclaim to a congressional committee visiting Riverside County, California, how Scripture compelled a tender concern for the Stephens' kangaroo rat and other endangered species. This speech—met with derisive laughter and jeers from the crowd assembled that had suffered mighty economic dislocation because of the rat, the California gnatcatcher, the Delhi Sands flower-loving fly, and the Riverside fairy shrimp, among other endangered species—did not advance the gospel or the environmentalist cause. Rather, this pastor was dismissed as a lightweight, probably between real jobs, and naive about how the law in question worked.

Ours is an era that demands credibility and credentials. Fame can sometimes substitute for these qualities, but not for long. If you are called by God to minister to the souls and needs of His people as a preacher or a pastor, expect to forfeit the ability to influence the world beyond your congregation. This may not be just. But it is fact.

There is one exception that must be noted. Scholars are different, even if their degrees are in theology or theology-related fields. If you would like to influence both the congregation and the non-church culture—if you must serve both—then stay within the academy at the end of your studies. There are some examples of such figures at work these days—Al Mohler of Southern Theological Seminary and J. P. Moreland of Biola University come to mind—but these are rare and extraordinarily talented intellects.

Generally the first rule is an inescapable rule. If you are ordained, leave the world to others, and tend to your flock. Both will be better served as a result.

CHAPTER 12

MOVE TO ONE OF THE THREE MAJOR CITIES

NO MATTER WHAT YOUR AGE, AND NO MATTER WHAT city you presently call home, you can make this choice today. At the very least review the choice you have made concerning an address, even if you cannot imagine moving.

The city you declare to be home is the most crucial of all the decisions you make when it comes to your career and the impact you will have upon the world. It is possible to affect any community, but only some communities can have a significant influence upon the country as a whole.

The three major centers of American life are New York, Washington, D.C., and Los Angeles. There are many other great cities, of course, but only these three are genuine crossroads in the life of the country. New York is the money; D.C. is the law; LA is the culture. And it is that simple.

The command and control structures of the three spheres are located in those cities. Intellectual life is spread among them (yes, even in California), but an ambition in one of those three areas obliges the holder of that ambition to head to one of the three sooner or later. And sooner is better.

I have lived in each of these cities, and in all of them before I hit twenty-five. To those younger than thirty, I encourage you to try to pull that off. Each place is so unique that knowledge of all of them is a key to effectiveness anywhere in the country.

But at a minimum, pick one and go there. Even if only for a few years. Even if you hate them all. Even if you have never lived with other than a rural address. America is a land of cities, and you cannot rise if you cannot handle at least one of the big three.

What do I mean by "handle"? To master the details of urban life, and to do so in a setting close to the real center of real power. In each of these three cities there is real, genuine, earthly power. People actually have it and use it. You can watch it. You can learn from watching. And the lessons are transferable.

Lessons learned in Chicago, by contrast, cannot be easily transferred. They are specific to that bustling city. The same is true of San Francisco, Denver, Phoenix, Cleveland, Houston, Atlanta, and on and on. Every day I talk to hundreds of thousands of people living in these cities, and they listen because the experiences gained and knowledge derived from my years in the big three are applicable everywhere. There is no major syndicated broadcaster or columnist who can work from other than one of the big three. It has not been done in recent years, and I doubt will ever be done again except by a rare, indeed extraordinary, individual. America has accepted this urban hierarchy grudgingly perhaps, but it has done so.

The good news is that each of these epicenters of power is hugely open to newcomers of all ages and talents, all backgrounds and skills sets. Each is so large as to need every type and to value every skill.

You can go there. Tomorrow. You won't starve. You'll find an apartment. You'll figure out the streets. (Well, maybe not the area around the Jefferson Memorial, but most places.) These are cities of new arrivers, by the millions, every decade.

Go. The greatest ambitions can be fulfilled only in these cities. Even lesser ambitions find the training available there to be the best.

Making your choice of a city, however, means making your choice between money, law, and culture. It is possible to impact all three spheres, but only as a by-product of first mastering one. If you have already decided that government draws you, and politics animates you, then your choice is easy. Off to the nation's capital you go.

But if you haven't decided anything beyond the conviction that you are called to serve the world via leadership in the world, start by thinking about those three spheres.

Two other notes. No matter where you are now, you can restart this process. If you are thirty-five and in middle management in Sacramento, you can restart this process.

Thousands do so every year. Even if you are married. Even if you have kids. Even if it involves risk. Even if your in-laws look at you as though you were from Mars. Even if your spouse agrees with your in-laws. And even if your kids don't want to change schools, much less states. People do it all the time.

But be sure of what you aspire to. If you want to lead at a state or a local level, the big three are tremendous assets in the training, but not absolutely necessary. There are elites at work in every community in the country, and people who have never spent more than a week in any of the big three will populate most of them.

Spend some time on this issue of national versus local leadership. The paths are very different. The former almost certainly requires time in New York, Washington, or Los Angeles. The latter merely gains a very useful, though not absolutely necessary, advantage from having done so.

CHAPTER 13

THE JOBS YOU WILL HAVE

PLAN ON AT LEAST ONE JOB EVERY THREE YEARS, AT least two jobs at the same time, and at least three jobs that turn out to be horrible.

The reality of the world of work is that most people do not like their jobs. In fact, most people hate them. As has been famously said, that's why they call it work.

This does not have to be your experience, however, if you adopt clear-eyed understandings about work.

First, recognize that you will make mistakes in your choice of employers. The interview process will trick you. You will misjudge the people, and you will misunderstand the position. Plus, people will lie to you. Often. You will be promised interesting work and rapid advancement, and instead you will get murderous hours doing incredibly boring tasks.

Second, realize that a job isn't a jail sentence. You can leave whenever you want to. Most people don't stay long enough to overcome the initial dissatisfaction and/or hazing, or they stay way too long. Almost every job deserves at least six months, but no terrible job ought to be endured even two years.

Third, understand that résumés with many jobs are much more interesting than résumés with one job. This is particularly true for people under the age of thirty-five in whom curiosity and drive are expected. Almost nothing counts against you before the age of thirty, and any number of job changes will be forgiven if your story is a good one.

Fourth, try to identify at least one long-term employee of every place you work who will say nice things about you if ever asked. Keep good records. Stay in touch. Make deposits in the favor bank for folks at work, during your time there and after you leave. Burning bridges and making dramatic exit speeches are for fools. Even the idiot in the next cubicle who played the music too loud and kept the AC on too high deserves a "good luck, see ya around" parting nod.

Fifth, look for the enormous learning opportunity built in to the job, and take advantage of it. The lowest-status employee in a newsroom is still in a newsroom, capable of observing and absorbing the rhythms and lessons of the place.

Sixth, if your stomach hurts on successive Sunday nights, the result of stress associated with Monday morning, quit. That is not normal. You will find another job. Everyone always finds another job. You won't starve, and you won't end up in the gutter. The folks in the gutter are not there because they quit a bad job.

Seventh, exit a job that does not come with a promotion

path clearly marked and a career path to climb. It can be fine for a year or two ride on the experience train, but if there is some chasm in front of you that you could never jump over, then don't stick around too long.

Eighth, if you can handle working for a successful jerk, do so for as long as you can tolerate it. Horrible bosses can make excellent teachers, even if they don't send you Christmas cards and even if they scream. Rent the movie *Swimming with the Sharks*. Your boss isn't so bad.

Ninth, prepare for a portfolio career. Most people have more than one source of income, and that means more than one job, though second jobs are difficult to manage and require some talent like writing, editing, or teaching. Keeping two careers going is fatiguing, but it is the best insurance policy against job disappointment.

Tenth, if you are lucky enough to find a mentor—the real, genuine deal, and not some puffed-up, mid-level suit looking for ego help—hang on to that mentor for as long as reasonably possible. Most acquaintances in the workplace are just that, acquaintances. They may have relationships with you of reciprocity, where they help you because you help them. They will not sacrifice for your benefit, and you should not expect them to. Indeed, competition is part of the workplace.

So if someone perceives in you a particular talent that deserves nurturing, or a set of skills that merits protection, and he extends you assistance, take it. Self-interest is at work at some level in the mentor in that situation, but self-interest is the common denominator of all workplaces. Sincere offers of assistance do come along. If you can identify and act upon the genuine article, you will gain a tremendous asset in your career.

Now for some don'ts. These are obvious, but time and again younger people forget them. To their regret.

Never steal from your employer. Not so much as a tablet.

Never date a fellow employee. Don't invite such invitations, and don't accept them.

Don't drink or otherwise party with the folks at the office. Occasionally a genuine friendship will sprout and grow in the office, but these are rare. Most out-of-office socializing is really office politics on location. Avoid it.

Don't speak ill of other employees. Period. It is, of course, contrary to the gospel to do so, and it is also always destructive of your situation. On a daily basis that will never stop, you will be invited to discuss the faults and shortcomings of your colleagues. Develop a habit of meeting every situation with an observation of the good side of the subject's work habits. Meet negative with positive at every turn. Some of the less talented will think you a Goody Two-shoes, but others will note your way of responding as evidence of maturity and diplomacy. It is both. The approval of some folks is not worth having.

Work hard and keep track of your accomplishments. No one else will. Defend your record against slander, and if you get stuck with a knucklehead of a boss, first try to educate him or her on your value. If it doesn't work, move on. There is rarely (if ever) an upside to anger in the workplace.

Finally, even if you are genuinely happy in your work, and even if you have a good boss and a clear career path marked out, always stay open to a new opportunity. Be ready to change within two weeks. A good job can always be succeeded by a perfect job, and a salary can always be increased. The office can get larger, the commute shorter, your colleagues more brilliant and engaging. In short, your contentment can become a mask that obscures even greater possibilities. Don't trust contentment; it anesthetizes ambition.

CHAPTER 14

THE NETWORKS YOU CHOOSE

IF YOU HAVE NOT ALREADY DONE SO, YOU WILL SOON BE doing an enormous amount of reading about network theory, a new branch of sociology that explores all of human life by examining the patterns of networks that exist and recur. Obvious networks include corporate boards, golf clubs, fund-raising organizations, and regular social gatherings. Network theory is the formal examination of the old cliché: "It's not what you know; it's who you know."

The academics are coming to the stunning conclusion that there is a lot of truth in that cliché. As the kid culture said for a few weeks in 1999 and adult culture repeated in 2000: "Well, hello?"

Clichés deserve attention because they are almost inevitably built on truth. So the question must be asked: Who do you know? To which you should respond: "What do you mean by *know*?"

There are many levels of knowing. You may know your neighbors well enough to grab the mail for each other during summer vacation. You may know your college roommate well enough to drop in for a visit when passing through town and even to assume the spare bedroom will be available to you. You may know your coworker well enough to cover for her when the boss is on a rampage or to advance a loan until payday.

You may know your spouse better than anyone in the world, yet not know one-thousandth of his or her childhood world. You may not know your pastor well enough to quickly recall his name when running into him out of the context of Sunday services, or that pastor may have walked alongside you through profound tragedy.

Knowing has a thousand meanings. In the world of ambition, its meaning is much more precise. You *know* someone when that individual can reliably be expected to assist you in the advance of your ambitions.

A wonderful *Washington Post* article in early 2002 detailed the dynamics of a truly inside-the-Beltway contest. The House of Representatives is organized hierarchically, and that pecking order exists in both the majority party and the minority party. Within the majority party, the leadership runs from the top job of Speaker of the House of Representatives to Majority Leader to Majority Whip. In the party with fewer votes, the chain runs from Minority Leader to Minority Whip and on down.

The Democrats became the minority party after the congressional elections of 1994. Since that time Richard Gephardt had led them, but in the fall of 2002 the position of Minority Whip became vacant due to the impending retirement of the incumbent David Bonior. Since Bonior's retirement had been expected for some time, the contest to replace him began in 1999. It was a race in which only Democratic members of the House had a vote, and with only 200-odd votes, it would take only 100 allies to win. Three candidates started the race, and when one of them, Georgia Democrat John Lewis, dropped out, the contest began in earnest between Nancy Pelosi, from California, and Steny Hoyer, from Maryland. Pelosi won. She had developed deeper ties with more Democratic congressmen; she knew more people.

Pelosi and Hoyer had laid their plans to run for this slot years before they actually asked their colleagues for votes. They built their networks over time, consciously and carefully cultivating acquaintances and then friendships. They *chose* their networks.

And so can you. You decide where you are going, and you identify who can help you get there. And then you endeavor to help them so that they might help you later. It is never an accident when elections or promotions are won or selections are made. Lottery winners are products of luck. Everyone else who advances had a plan and stuck to it.

Pelosi, by the way, went on to become the first woman to ever lead either party caucus in either chamber of Congress. She was elected leader of the Democrats in the House in November 2002—another victory she owed to her cultivation of her network.

· CHAPTER 15 ·

Choosing the People You Will Work For

When you are under thirty, seek jobs that put you in close contact with leaders. Pass up a big-name company or firm for the opportunity to work closely with a leader of a small firm or company. If you are in government, it is much better to be the personal assistant to an assistant secretary than it is to have control of an office of thirty people buried in the bowels of a bureaucracy. The money hardly matters at all early in your career. Your early jobs are about finding career-long sponsors, and those folks *never* notice the basement colonels.

The military understands the value of matching young officers with generals and admirals, and an elaborate system of military aides exists to provide that value. Most political people understand the dynamics as well.

Richard Nixon always understood the value of mixing youth into his leadership team. The upside of the approach, as well as the danger, was loyalty to the leader that set the standard—until James Carville and Paul Begala appeared on the scene.

In his exile Nixon drafted young professionals to work in close quarters with him.

I was one. John Taylor, Paul Bateman, and Monica Crowley were others. Nearly a decade after his death, these are four people who knew Nixon professionally and can still speak to his real views and thoughts from firsthand experience. Nixon quite consciously constructed a network of long-lived experts on him.

At every level from the Oval Office to the smallest city hall, constant training is under way. People with power and talent are always seeking to expand their networks, and the easiest way to do this is to credential young people of talent. In every profession of influence there are opportunities to join the team of an accomplished individual. Take them.

Jeff Greenfield of CNN fame wrote a forgettable book a long way back, from which I remember only one thing. (I have even forgotten the title.) Greenfield counseled young people in or around politics (and this includes the media) to seek out a sponsor of the sort described above, to hitch up to the wagon, and to never let go.

We disagree on this last point. The military limits the duration of its aide assignments for a reason, and young people should as well. Four years max, I think—though two are often better and even one year may be acceptable—can do the trick of gaining insight and sponsorship. Lifelong aides can never make the jump to genuine influence of their own, and their stars will diminish as their sponsors' do if they do not jump ship after their apprenticeship.

The question a young reader is asking—or should be—is, "How do I get such a job in the first place?" There is no great science here, simply the intersection of diligent searching and luck.

If you have taken the time throughout college and graduate school to cultivate friendships with adults in a variety of settings—professors with past government experience, candidates for office, administrators—you should now present them with a request: Do they know anybody of influence to whom you could apply for a year's internship at low pay? If you pose this question to enough people (and friends of friends count), doors will open. Keep knocking. The key is limiting your desire for income and tenure.

Of course, if you have spent four to seven years drinking beer and suddenly have an itch to rise, you are at a considerable disadvantage. The young men and women who were scrambling to help arrange conferences, run campaigns, conduct the continuing education registration seminar, and more, will have a considerable head start on you.

Because I am primarily interested in government and politics, I want to pause here to offer specific advice on the subject of rising in the world of politics and government.

I landed on Nixon's small personal staff in 1978 because I took a job researching for his son-in-law, David Eisenhower. Notice of that opportunity came because I sought an interview with an author and former White House speechwriter, Ray Price, who originally thought he might need a research assistant. Instead he connected me to David. I had heard of Ray's potential need from an undergraduate friend, Ed Mansfield, whom I chanced to pass on a street in Cambridge and with whom I spent less than five minutes talking. Of such chance conversations—*and the willingness to act upon the hint of opportunity*—are careers made.

Ray was willing to talk to me, I think, because I combined academics with a record. I had spent hours and hours in campaigns in 1974 and 1976, first for Republican Congressman Paul Cronin, who was defeated by Paul Tsongas in the Watergate-inspired massacre of congressional Republicans in 1974, and later for the Ford presidential campaign (a forlorn experience in Massachusetts) in 1976. Campaigns are the great markers of bona fides, and every two years any young person with serious political ambition should be toiling away on one of them. Even when the work is dull and repetitious, and even when you see the candidate only a handful of times.

Washington, D.C., like Hollywood, will yield to young people of ambition and energy, though not quickly, and perhaps not in the manner you had thought. The paths are circuitous and bumpy, but they are there.

The other professions also hold to traditions. There are ways to rise in large law firms and big hospitals, in consulting firms, and in the media. Usually you will need a powerful sponsor in your early years, but not to be your friend. No, your aim is to impress with ability and work ethic, so much so that when you decide to move on, he will gladly make the call to his counterpart somewhere else and effect your transition.

One additional note: the next time you have the chance to talk with an individual of accomplishment, ask her how she got where she is. And then listen and probe for a lesson in ambition (and you might also hear of some pretty interesting potential connections for yourself). Very few successful people resent being asked to detail their rise, although the circumstances have to be appropriate to having such a conversation.

Be sure, as well, to learn to keep notes on these talks. I cannot remember Greenfield's book, but I can find in a moment just about every colleague with whom I have worked closely for the past quarter century. The favors I ask for now I ask for other people, but the ability to make the call depends upon the discipline to keep track of where people are.

CHAPTER 16

UNLESS YOU OWN THE COMPANY, YOU CAN BE REPLACED

WHEN I DID MY FIRST RADIO BROADCAST IN DECEMBER of 1990, the station I had joined, KFI AM 640, had begun a long domination of the news-talk format in the toughest radio market in the world, Los Angeles. The anchor of the lineup that had brought the station to prominence was Tom Leykis, a self-styled libertarian whose combination of vulgar humor and theatrics had driven the ratings north. Tom thought that he was the most talented radio guy in LA, and a lot of people agreed with him. He began to act as though he were indispensable.

No one is indispensable. Tom was fired suddenly, and the amazement around the station was complete. How could management do that? The answer is simply because it was management. It could do whatever it wanted.

Christians are supposed to know that pride is the deadliest sin—the sin of Lucifer, the sin of every would-be messiah and false prophet that history has ever thrown up. Pride stalks successful individuals, shadowing them and setting them up for a fall in their careers and for estrangement from God.

There is a long list readily available for anyone to study on the limits of talent and the suddenness of fortune's shift. The best example from the last twenty-five years is the rise and very sudden and complete fall of Secretary of State Al Haig. The general-turned-statesman thought he could run Ronald Reagan, but Ronald Reagan ran the general right out of the State Department. When Haig threatened to resign, Reagan said okay. End of Haig. He wasn't indispensable.

You will be tempted often to think that you are the key to any organization and that no one would dare cross you or contradict you, much less fire you. When you begin to believe that, you have entered the most dangerous path of your career. At that moment, consider the virtue of humility. Because you are about to be shown the door.

When this happens to you, and it will happen to a lot of readers of this book because it is a marked pattern in the lives of the talented and ambitious, remember to do a few things.

First, speak only good things about the people who bounced you. There is no upside in bitterness, and a great deal of recovery from a fall begins with graciousness.

Second, hang on to the fact that nothing is ever a career ender unless you had already reached the summit of your profession.

Third, ask yourself whether, in eternity's scheme, the throttling of pride via an unceremonious exit is the best thing that could have happened to you. If you really believe in the infinite trajectory of souls, the knockdown in this life that produces humility is much to be preferred to the knockdown in the next that produces separation from God for eternity.

Nevertheless, humility on the front end is easier than after a big bounce. Getting and keeping humility depend upon two things: genuine appreciation of the talents of others, especially those in your field, and Christ's message of radical equality.

The first approach is pragmatic. Fix your eye on folks in your field who have done far better than you. For every broadcast journalist in America there is Rush Limbaugh with six hundred stations and twenty million daily listeners to dwarf their own following or platform. No one can claim to be the best in the business because Rush is the best in the business, regardless of your political view or your taste for the show. That's why I listen to Rush at least a bit every day; he is the standard. Folks who succeed in broadcasting by dint of the critical mass they inherited, like Tom Brokaw, Dan Rather, and Peter Jennings, are not to be compared to a pioneer, and their achievements, though significant, don't include invention of the form. So find a model of incredible success, and focus on the distance between you and him.

But even more effective is Christ's rejection of hierarchy. He told His closest followers that the first among them would be the last and the last, first. This should be a daily meditation for people seeking power and influence. It is not a prediction; it is a guarantee. Jesus will elevate the poorest and least powerful in the next life. He will be hard on the powerful who are indifferent to suffering, and who use their position only for themselves:

There was a certain rich man who was clothed in purple and fine linen and fared sumptuously every day. But there was a certain beggar named Lazarus, full of sores, who was laid at his gate, desiring to be fed with the crumbs which fell from the rich man's table. Moreover the dogs came and licked his sores. So it was that the beggar died, and was carried by the angels to Abraham's bosom. The rich man also died and was buried. And being in torments in Hades, he lifted up his eyes and saw Abraham afar off, and Lazarus in his bosom. Then he cried and said, "Father Abraham, have mercy on me, and send Lazarus that he may dip the tip of his finger in water and cool my tongue; for I am tormented in this flame." But Abraham said, "Son, remember that in your lifetime you received your good things, and likewise Lazarus evil things; but now he is comforted and you are tormented. And besides all this, between us and you there is a great gulf fixed, so that those who want to pass from here to you cannot, nor can those from there pass to us." Then he said, "I beg you therefore, father, that you would send him to my father's house, for I have five brothers, that he may testify to them, lest they also come to this place of torment." Abraham said to him, "They have Moses and the prophets; let them hear them." And he said, "No, father Abraham; but if one goes to them from the dead, they will repent." But he said to him, "If they do not hear Moses and the prophets, neither will they be persuaded though one rise from the dead." (Luke 16:19–31)

For those in authority, with power and influence, this teaching of Jesus is one of the most terrible passages in all of Scripture, for it confirms not only the existence of hell and the awfulness of the place, but also the dangers of power and the sheer deafness of those whom the world elevates. Christ underscored that hardly any warning can penetrate the world of the rich and the powerful, not even warnings from dead men risen again.

And this is why the unexpected fall from power can so often have a transforming effect on the one who takes a nose-dive. Suddenly he begins to hear again and is obliged by circumstance to abandon the pride that deafens him to this message and the other messages of the gospel.

It would be better not to have to learn humility the hard way. The best way to avoid that sudden fall is to keep your betters in ability, and your equals in worth, like Lazarus, in mind.

CHAPTER 17

KNOW WHAT YOU DON'T KNOW

THE MOST SUCCESSFUL PEOPLE I KNOW HAVE NEVER been afraid to recognize superior skill in others, no matter the type of skill and no matter the other. The ability to recognize superior skill allowed them the opportunity to milk advantage from observing that skill.

Example: historian and author Gary Wills is one of the most impressive and prolific popular historians/public intellectuals of our time. Because I understand his gifts, I'll grab his books even though I am almost certain to disagree with his conclusions in most political matters.

Thus when writing this book, I picked up his new one, *Why I Am a Catholic,* and learned from it that the English writer G. K. Chesterton had written a book on Dickens. ("When at Campion, I had read Chesterton's book on Charles Dickens, and it made me plow through the Dickens novels in chronological order.") I love Dickens, and because I'm willing to follow Wills's trail, I came upon a fact I did not know and perhaps an entry into Chesterton, whose work has never appealed to me the way it does to others.

Which explains perfectly, I hope, why attending an Angels game with broadcaster and former Reds pitcher Frank Pastore was so much fun for me, or why I prefer Lakers games with my broadcast partner of many years, Kerman Maddox, who played an excellent game in high school and eats and breathes Lakers. Or why I like to interview Dennis Prager or Michael Medved on Israel or Frank Gaffney on missile defense. I love learning from experts. You should as well.

The hardest words for some people to learn to say or write are "I don't know." So I recommend practicing. Try to add, "In fact, I don't have a clue," whenever you can. These phrases will open up huge opportunities for you.

You will benefit from the learning that comes your way from this frank admission of ignorance; it is also among the most disarming and authentic responses in modern times. It is so rarely heard, this admission of ignorance, that it carries a huge impact. This simple admission will earn you increased credibility.

The fellow who is quick to admit what he doesn't know is much more likely to be believed when he asserts his expertise.

Consider it an excellent day when you can ask an expert for his or her guidance.

CHAPTER 18

Make Frequent Deposits in the Favor Bank

You ought to read Tom Wolfe's *The Bonfire of the Vanities,* but you probably won't. Younger Americans do not read novels of the '80s anymore, certainly not books of the heft of *Bonfire.* And as the movie made from the book was so awful and thus so unrented, the book has been obscured as well by time's march to the sea.

It is a good read, though, as a telescope back to the era that spawned you: the early years of the first age when large sums of money were controlled by young people who had not been raised up within families used to controlling great wealth and thus accomplished in how to teach the appropriate ways of using such wealth. The eighties were very much the first era when significant numbers of people under forty had and spent large incomes. The effect was delirium—first phase of the fever that eventually swept an entirely new generation in the dotcom years.

Wolfe captured the variety and the excess, but he also artic-ulated a phrase that still has currency among some sociologists with style. You should memorize it and the truths it conveys: "the favor bank."

Wolfe's two key characters are a rich, young Wall Street investment banker in trouble with the law and his streetwise, combative middle-class defense lawyer. The latter can assure the former of a smoother ride through the bumpy criminal courts because the lawyer has, throughout his career, been faithfully making deposits in "the favor bank." He's been doing favors for people, and they owe him favors in return. He can withdraw favors because he deposited many over the years.

So should you. Often, if you can. Occasionally, more than one per day. Deposit making in the favor bank is the critical ingredient to rising in the world.

I am not talking here about Christian duties that ought to be done because we are commanded by Christ to feed the hungry, clothe the naked, and give water to the thirsty, shelter to the homeless, and comfort to prisoners. These obligations are real and vast, and they may overlap in part with the self-interested maintenance of a healthy balance in the favor bank. But favor-bank deposits spring from motives that have nothing in common with following Christ, though they are not hostile to following Christ. They are parallel paths.

Deposits in the favor bank are the help you extend to those who might help you in the future. The bargain is not explicit. To discuss the bargain is, in fact, to void it in most cases. Rather, you lend a hand in the expectation that you will need a hand. And you do so indiscriminately because the assist you may need in the future is as unknowable today as is the agency of its delivery ten years from now.

"Help unlooked for" is a fine phrase conjuring up the image of the cavalry coming over the hill just as the battle is about to go the way of the enemy. But "help unlooked for" is typically the very, very, very rare exception to the rule that help can reasonably be expected only from those you yourself have helped, or the friends of those you yourself have helped. It's a linked chain. And the more links you forge by generously doing favors, the more you build an iron coat of potential benefit.

Like your real bank account, your balance in the favor bank ought to be drawn down only when there is a real need. Let it accumulate interest. Let it compound. Don't call in favors when you don't need them. Move your own apartment against the day you'll need to get a friend sprung from jail in a distant city. If you go to the well often, there will be zero water before too long.

CHAPTER 19

SUCCESS IS NOT ZERO-SUM, SO PROMOTE THE SUCCESS OF OTHERS

MANY PROFESSIONALS, BUT ESPECIALLY THOSE IN POLITICS, see success as a zero-sum game. A zero-sum game is one in which for every win, there must be a loss; from every triumph, a defeat.

Sports are usually zero-sum. Every time a win goes in one team's column, a loss goes into some other team's record.

Many situations in life are zero-sum. But success in the world is rarely that way. There are rare situations where two people must compete, like a presidential election, but that is far from typical. The much more usual situation is clustered triumph, when entire organizations succeed, generally because of the efforts of scores of talented people.

You will be tempted, especially early in your career, to resent the triumphs of others. This is jealousy, and it lurks in every ambitious heart. It's the green-eyed beast, but it can be tamed and ultimately defeated via the combination of scriptural teaching, habit, and self-interest.

The standard comes from Scripture. Although the apostles

often disagreed and even openly competed on one occasion (which drew the rebuke of Christ), the vast bulk of the Acts of the Apostles is devoted to charting efforts of all on behalf of all. Clearly you are called to encourage and assist in the success of others' ministries and just as clearly in the success of others' careers.

This is much easier said than done. Where many might understand the concept of the favor bank, they are positively trained to compete against peers in the same fields, and that is especially true in the professions. The *Paper Chase* movie endures as a popular rental among about-to-begin-law-school types because it accurately portrays the sometimes desperate attempts to excel when the competition is extraordinary. I imagine that the atmosphere is much the same within medical and business schools and certainly among athletes competing for a roster spot.

There is no denying the fierce competition for entry-level positions in any meritocracy, and elbows can be very sharp indeed. Once you're inside any door, however, the key to life-long success is a habit of helping others through that very same door or through other portals to opportunity.

I cannot stress this point enough. Every time you give an assist to another's career, you advance your own. Each time you sacrifice time or effort on another's behalf, you do so for yourself as well.

Not that you won't be met with ingratitude. Ingratitude in this world is like oxygen—one of the basic elements of life.

But if you help hundreds of people, the odds are quite good that most will be grateful allies in your own ambition. We are back at the favor bank again, but in a highly specialized area—the promotion of would-be rivals.

The favor bank is an easy-enough concept to understand because it is so obviously transactional. You give and you get in a clear way, even though the accounting is less than exact.

But promoting rivals? Helping someone who could conceivably edge you out? That's career suicide, or so you would think. But it's not. Indeed, at the highest levels it is the mark of the most successful people.

Every assist you give to a potential rival is, in fact, an investment in your career. Most people do not forget such assists. Most people understand reciprocity. Indeed, most good people will feel obligation as a result of assistance received.

And you will almost certainly strengthen your organization by promoting talent, and the highest levels notice such things.

A few years back, a commercial depicted a group of executives attempting to solve a supply shortage of a critical manufacturing material. The Internet-savvy youngster worked his laptop and identified a supply that the older, slower execs had speculated could not be found. The gruff CEO nodded surprise approval at the kid as he walked from the room, and also thanked another participant in the meeting, who was obviously shocked by the compliment. "What'd I do?" he asked. "You hired Johnson [the kid]," came the reply.

Although the ad guys played this for a laugh, they exposed

a real dynamic; the talent scout is a key player in every organization, and the thanks he gets are not typically flippant.

The CEO of every organization has very few tasks, and a truly key one is finding talent. It requires the technical ability to understand the job that must be filled as well as an eye for character. I think the latter is by far the harder to develop.

Having an eye for character means having the gift of discernment—the ability to see through a résumé and into an applicant, and to appreciate subtle skills. The best managers and professionals are always promoting others, not themselves, so it takes extra effort to find the creative thinker and the disciplined implementer if both folks are intent on promoting their subordinates.

The best leaders have that eye because they have spent a professional career developing talent and watching it grow. Not without mistakes, sometimes big ones. But usually with results that replicate and form patterns.

The inability to judge character will eventually disable your career because success means finding colleagues and staff, lawyers and accountants. If you can't figure out how to do this, you will be at a loss to take your individual talent and multiply its effects.

The sooner you begin to do this, the more practice and thus the more success you will have.

Now a caution.

There is always a temptation to advance the careers of friends, and certainly if friends are qualified, there is good reason to do just that. The desire to do good things for friends is the essence of friendship, and assisting in friends' careers is a fine aspiration.

Provided, of course, that you are not assisting them into failure.

An easy example. Think of all your friends who golf. Now think of the one who is worst among them. This is where I live, in the land of the twenty-plus handicaps.

A friend of mine who signed me up to play in a Pro-Am tournament would be no friend for long. The fun of meeting Tiger, Phil, or David would quickly dissolve in the stress of quadruple bogies and out-of-bounds. I am not designed for Pro-Am golf.

Promoting unqualified individuals into positions for which they are not prepared will lead to their failure. Bad for them. Bad for you. Don't do it.

But do not become overcautious in the assessment of talent. If a friend *might* be able to pull off an assignment, discuss it with him, being careful to explain the risks as well as the rewards. Everyone needs a break now and again. Be on the giving end of your fair share.

CHAPTER 20

DISCLOSE THE WEAK POINTS IN YOUR ARGUMENT AND DEAL WITH THEM

A COMMON MISTAKE AMONG PROFESSIONALS ON THE rise is the attempt to shield the weak points in their positions. Too often the temptation is indulged to avoid the toughest question or the most difficult problem. This is not lying, and the behavior is not necessarily immoral, but it is almost never prudent. The best advocates anticipate and meet the strongest objections to their arguments rather than hope opponents will not raise them or superiors will not see them.

"Logistics win wars"—this is a common saying, and nothing is more crucial than food and water for an army on the march. This is the toughest problem for most generals who have faced long campaigns against determined foes.

Such problems are not dealt with on the fly, and they are not postponed until the end. The toughest puzzles are solved first, allowing the limits imposed by those solutions to define the boundaries of the possible. You can't march on Berlin without enough gasoline, a problem that will not disappear, no matter how many Pattons are in command.

An ambitious man will encounter a hundred situations where he will be called upon to present superiors with options. An ambitious woman will daily have to provide advice to levels of management who depend on her briefings. Each would-be riser must always be careful to inform fully of risks and rewards, even if he has identified his own recommended course of action.

Here is a lesson I teach all my law students.

Because a court is obliged to follow the decisions of higher courts, a judge reads casebooks for cases similar to the one he is currently considering. This is called the search for binding precedent.

Lawyers on both sides of a case help the judge by filing papers with the court that bring relevant cases to the judge's attention. The lawyer spends hours and hours researching old cases to find the ones most closely resembling the situation of his client in which the side most resembling the situation of his client won. Then the lawyer argues to the court that the court is bound to follow that case and rule for his client.

Since there are literally hundreds of thousands of cases already decided with their decisions already published, this hunt for precedent can be exhausting and complicated. The papers filed with courts—called briefs—can be huge and can point to hundreds of cases where courts considered similar situations.

The lawyer will often find cases that look very much like his case, yet the earlier court ruled against the people who look very much like that lawyer's current client. These are the facts of life for a lawyer: there are almost always some cases that hurt your argument.

I always lead my students to highlight these cases. "Hanging a lantern on your problem" is an old saying in politics. "Hang a lantern on bad precedent," I lecture and lecture and lecture.

Nothing is harder for a lawyer to overcome than a judge who believes she has been misled or only partially informed by that lawyer. If the decision maker is going to be fair, and almost all judges in the American system will comply with precedent when it fits, there is only peril in keeping the court in the dark about disadvantageous precedent.

There is an ethical obligation for lawyers to disclose all relevant cases to a court, and only the ethically impaired will fail to do so. But there are vast differences between an unhelpful case mentioned in a footnote and one that is highlighted and discussed candidly and at length in a prominent place in a lawyer's brief.

As with the best lawyers, so with the best leaders in all fields: assess your strengths and weaknesses with objective and thorough analysis, and put your biggest problems in the center of the table.

Put the hardest issue at the top of the agenda.

There are some exceptions to this rule, and they typically involve situations where decision makers are biased or unfair, or when, as happens in the law frequently, you are called to

defend your client's interests and are under no ethical obligation to disclose harmful facts. Even in those circumstances it is
sometimes useful to disclose bad facts or troubling problems.

The tendency to postpone grappling with the hardest
problems and the most difficult choices is deeply ingrained in
our culture that frowns on negative thinking. But there is no
wishing away the big decisions and no inventing solutions
from thin air. An ability to focus on the toughest challenges
is an advantage for your career and for your company.

CHAPTER 21

ALWAYS BE PREPARED TO ADMIT ERROR, AND MOST OF THE TIME, KEEP THAT ADMISSION TO YOURSELF

IF YOU INSIST ON ALWAYS HAVING BEEN RIGHT, YOU WILL, of course, be wrong, and your colleagues and friends will know this. The gracious among them will refer to you as "stubborn," and the less gentle will brand you a fool.

Two examples: the Fonz and Pope Gregory.

In the 1970s, the *Happy Days* character the Fonz began one of the quintessential American television runs. For a period of two or three years, this cycle-riding throwback became an icon—a sort of ideal of young American manhood. The Henry Winkler role was not intended to dominate the series, but it quickly did and then dominated American television for many years (until Fonzie "jumped the shark"—an episode of such astonishing stupidity that it gave rise to its own cultural label: "jumping the shark," which now means the moment when a popular phenomenon is recognized as spent, as *over*).

During his heyday, the Fonz was always right, and he always saved the program's other characters from a variety of perils. One memorable episode was built around Fonzie's screwup. He had to admit, "I was wrong." Never having said it, he could not get the words out easily, and it took many tries before Fonzie could come to grips with this capacity for error and actually saying, "I was wrong."

The humor, of course, is that everyone has this capacity for error, and we all engage it often, probably daily. The idea of anyone never having had to say, "I was wrong," was the punch line. It was an absurd premise, possible only in a sitcom.

Pope Gregory I, a leader of the early church, had to lend a hand to one of his predecessors as pope, Pelagius II. In 585, Pelagius II had to explain that a couple of earlier popes had screwed up. It was a delicate task, given that the admission of error was seen then as now as a dangerous display of vulnerability. So Pelagius turned to his aide Gregory, and Gregory ghosted this explanation (in *Why I Am a Catholic* by Garry Wills):

> Since Peter contradicted himself, should you tell him, "We refuse to hear what you are saying because you once said the opposite?" If . . . one position was held while truth was being sought, and a different position was adopted after truth had been found, why should a change of position be considered a crime . . .? [O]ne should not blame a change in one's stand but the inability to take a stand. So if the mind is firmly intent on seeking the truth, why will you criticize it when it sheds ignorance and fashions a better statement of the truth?

So many young professionals refuse to accept Gregory's

advice or the absurdity of the Fonz. In fact, they attempt—unconsciously, of course—to project a Fonz-like record of perfection that unwittingly tends to make them appear absurd.

There is no admission of ignorance in a confession of error. My lines are always open for people who interject stories of how they have screwed up or how they have blundered. Not only is it great evidence of an active, curious, and growing intellect, but it is great evidence of genuine self-confidence.

Developing the ability to quickly recognize errors in your actions, plans, or character is an insurance policy against career-destroying stubbornness. Imagine where Coke would be had it persisted in its New Coke folly. People blunder. Even the best, most innovative, most trustworthy folks blunder.

Now for a crucial bit of clarity: not every error needs to be admitted and not every screwup requires public confession. This is an area where Christians can confuse the pattern of the Christian life—wherein moral failings do require confession and repentance—with failings in the world, which carry no moral weight.

The world is awash in confession nowadays, though not typically of a particularly penitent sort. This has caught on in celebrity circles, especially with regard to admissions of chemical abuse or intolerance of this or that group of the month.

Most of the people you will call boss in the course of your life do not need to know about your screwups if those screwups have been reversed, resolved, and contained. Most of these people will be intensely grateful never to hear from you about your shortcomings if the shortcomings do not in any material way affect their ability to lead, manage, or produce.

Please consider the mail room.

I worked in a mail room throughout my senior year at Harvard. When I first grabbed the job, it was a shock because the mail room opened at 6:30 A.M. I had never seen 6:30 A.M. through three-plus years as an undergrad. (Later, when I did fifteen months as a "morning drive" talk show host, I discovered 4:15 A.M. This is an even greater shock to the system. So, too, is the recognition that an entire world exists around the clock, and the 4:15 America is the hardest-working America of them all.)

I would stumble into Harvard's Mount Holyoke Center Mail Room at 6:30 A.M. and begin to sort the morning mail with John, the local guy who stayed year in and year out. In my first month I made hundreds of errors, and mail went to wrong addresses with almost as much regularity as it did to the correct slot. In the second month I improved dramatically, and in the third month, John even took a few days off.

Not once did John consider it necessary to know which mail I had misdirected or the volume of errors. He didn't need to know that; he assumed I was making a prodigious number of mistakes.

I am certain that John's boss—I never met him—knew neither that I was there nor that I made errors. In short, had I bothered anyone up the organization with a catalog of my shortcomings, I would have been adding to his burden and not contributing to the organization.

The vast, vast majority of workplace errors you will make matter as much as my misdirected mail. They are the ordinary casualties of a learning curve's length, and no great moral dilemma arises from them.

There are the errors of every profession, whether doctoring, lawyering, pastoring, or building vast structures. Rarely—I mean really rarely—do your screwups matter. So spare your superiors the lengthy accounts of your setbacks and triumphs. They do not need to know, and thus they do not want to know.

CHAPTER 22

KNOW WHOM YOU OWE

WHEN I DEBATED JAMES CARVILLE AT ASPEN'S HOTEL Jerome in the summer of 1992, he had not yet become a cartoon. A decade ago he was a maverick political strategist with an indecipherable accent and a devilish smile. We were standing at the bar, and he was telling me about Harris Wofford's campaign for Pennsylvania's Senate seat. Wofford had won an upset in 1990, and Carville's handling of the campaign and his use of the health care issue catapulted him to the center of the national stage. Bill Clinton signed him up, gave him the role of Best Supporting Actor in a Presidential Campaign, and Carville never looked back.

Most of Carville's glory lay ahead of him in the summer of 1992. He could still walk through airports without being stopped. He would still agree to debates with conservative tomato cans like me before the Democratic Governors' Association (DGA) because his boss, Clinton, needed him to show up and keep the energy going. This was prior to the convention and the on-again-off-again-on-again campaign of

Ross Perot and the first President Bush's disastrous debate in the round. Clinton was no sure thing in the long summer days of 1992, and Carville was there to help.

I was there as a favor to an old friend, Mark Gearan. Mark is among my handful of closest friends, and he was helping guide the Clinton candidacy. (Eventually he'd be deputy chief of staff and communications director in the White House and director of the Peace Corps, but at that point he was running the DGA.) Mark has an eye for a show, and he knew Carville was at his best with a foil, so he called on me, local talent from the Los Angeles television and radio market, to play the bobo doll in Carville's act.

The debate that day didn't matter a whit. Just entertainment. But I confess I liked Carville because he was very much an original, and there aren't many originals in American politics.

Over the years, Carville morphed into something very different, or rather, he divided himself. On the one hand, he was Mary Matalin's husband, and Mary Matalin is a superb thinker and wonderful human being. They obviously love each other, so there is a James Carville we don't see.

Then there is the Carville we do see: the rasping, cutting, snapping, snarling, sometimes frothy, and occasionally incoherent villain of the cable shows and stump speeches. Even as a performer of political vaudeville, he can repel even the most hard-edged operatives. Carville's savaging of Ken Starr was a low point in American political history. His new role on CNN's *Crossfire* hasn't mellowed him.

What happened to Carville? His loyalty got the better of his judgment. His loyalty twisted him and his priorities. It became a horrible mutation of a very high and noble virtue. And it is an excellent way to begin a review of debt.

This chapter is intended as a crucial reminder for everyone. It is intended to spark in all readers a recollection of exactly who gave them a break, provided a push, or offered a hand up after a nasty fall. American culture generally does not encourage gratitude toward or even recognition of those who made success possible. From this gratitude gap come enormous consequences, most of which are negative, including vanity and self-absorption.

When was the last time you privately credited someone with contributing to all or part of your success? We watch stylized thank-yous pour out of Oscar winners each year, and this ritual seems to have infiltrated our culture: at the moment of stunning and undeniable achievement, we tend to spend a moment or two on thank-yous. Then it is move-on time, a ritual completed and the next challenge beckoning.

Genuine gratitude is of a different texture altogether, and it begins with internal recognition of those who make daily life possible. There are legions of people who are cooperating to make every minute of each one of your days possible. Some are working quite hard, like a trucker on the road at 3:00 A.M. to deliver produce for separation and shipment to the mega food market near you, or the crossing guard who protects your children, your neighbor's children, the children of your extended family, and even you from the tragedy you might otherwise be a part of. There is a pastor at work in his study preparing a sermon that will lift your eyes, and there is a research scientist on a stool in a lab working not on the drug that will save you today, but on a drug that will buy you a half dozen more years when you are old and enjoying your grandchildren.

There are sailors on the bridge of ships half a globe and twelve hours ahead of you, standing watch on a world, many parts of which would prefer you and millions of Americans dead. There are rough men on drilling platforms extracting oil so that you can drive where you wish, and there are engineers in broadcast booths the country over providing the news you want, the analysis you need, and sometimes the entertainment you deserve.

Somewhere a novelist is suffering through a rewrite or a historian through an editor's slashing remarks to give you insight, facts, or both.

And there are your receptionist, secretary, and gardener, the car-wash staff, the restaurant cook, the waiter, the dishwasher, and the trash collector.

Not to mention your spouse, and if you have them, your kids.

And that's just today's set of thank-yous.

Someone nursed you, clothed you, kept you safe. Not everyone can say that. Millions die before they draw a breath. Millions more before the age of five. Millions more are beaten, abused, famished, and diseased.

Someone taught you to read, gave you music, showed you a sport.

Someone inspired you to learn, told you about God, introduced you to your spouse, granted you an interview, gave you a job.

Someone assisted your dad; someone helped your spouse; someone coached your daughter.

And someone will bring you a blanket in a hospital room, give you a ride to a doctor's appointment, and hold your hand as death approaches.

Our utter dependence on others is so obvious and so complete that it is as invisible as oxygen and just as necessary.

You've got to know whom you owe. When you do, you'll have a perspective that allows for happiness, indeed, makes happiness inevitable. Concentration on the absolute quantity of assistance you have received in the past and are receiving now should quiet and dispel dissatisfaction.

The annual spring break for tens of thousands of high school students in California means a mission trip to Mexico, usually with the goal of building a house for a Mexican family living in extraordinarily harsh circumstances. For more than a dozen years, I have heard teenagers speak to my church the Sunday following their return. It is always the same talk, and it is always inspiring. These young people have been to a developing country and have seen genuine poverty. They are moved by the privation they witness. And they are profoundly grateful for their own circumstances, family, and country upon their return. For at least a brief moment, they are genuinely grateful.

But I am not sure they know whom they owe. Certainly they return thanking God, which is an essential recognition of God's sovereignty. But their grasp on why they enjoy plenty and why Mexicans are mired in want is limited. Do you suppose it occurs to them that their plenty is the result not just of their parents' love and work, but of the love and work of generations of ancestors?

Is this a homily of gratitude? You betcha, as they say in Minnesota. It is worth an entire book, this subject, but two chapters will do, for no one cares for the subject all that much.

Knowing whom you owe is a tricky business, which is why I began this chapter with Carville. I suspect Carville disfigured his public presence because of too much gratitude toward Clinton—the fella who gave him the big break, the guy who brought him to the dance. In fact, Carville wrote an entire book on the subject of loyalty, titled *Stickin'*, which is an apology for his ferocity.

Gratitude, like everything else, can be overdone.

But there is much more danger in too little gratitude than in too much.

Compare Carville, with all his many faults, with Dick Morris, the most repellent figure in American politics. Clinton made Morris as well, but when Morris self-destructed, he rebuilt his career by attacking Clinton and especially Hillary. I am no fan of the senator from New York and I frequently criticize her on my program, but I owe her nothing. Morris is simply a blackguard, but unfortunately he is also an emblem of our times—an opinion Hessian, like corporate Hessians and theological Hessians and entertainment Hessians.

At every level of American society this disregard for obligations based upon gratitude for past service or kindness is evident. A-Rod is with the Rangers, Shaq with the Lakers, and Barry Sanders is retired because—unlike Ripkin—they judged themselves without obligations to the Mariners, the Magic, and the Lions, respectively. Writers, actors, anchors, and musicians move from deal to deal without so much as a look back. I wrote the first draft of this chapter the week after Cornell West attempted to dress up his leaving Harvard for Princeton as some sort of payback to Harvard's new president.

It often seems that nobody owes anyone anything. Except that everyone does.

Know whom you owe. Know that you owe. You're fooling yourself if you think you made it or will make it on your own.

CHAPTER 23

FILL THE GRATITUDE GAP

IN THE PRECEDING CHAPTER, I REMINDED YOU OF THE debts that you owe others. Now I'd like to prompt you to act on that recognition. Make a list of the folks you owe. Do it in the margin. Do it now.

Start with family, and keep in mind that even a pain-in-the-neck sister may have been the key to your happiness via a sacrifice you have chosen to forget or a favor long forgotten.

Then move chronologically. There's a reason why most people can name every one of their teachers: each one impacts them in deep and inescapable ways. Some of these impacts are profoundly negative. But others change the trajectory of a person's life to a better and higher arc.

There's a reason why the movie *Stand and Deliver* inspired. We know that there is a great truth in the ability of a teacher to change lives. Pick up any presidential memoir and see if the writer does not pause to name at least one teacher.

Jay Mathews, the education writer for the *Washington Post*, wrote a column singing the praises of high school guidance counselors. After I read it on the air, the reaction was extraordinary. Caller after caller phoned in to echo Mathews's generic praise with a specific account of the help given them by a guidance counselor.

Coaches figure prominently in the lists of indebtedness I have seen.

Teachers. Coaches. Then mentors and friends. These are the geological layers of your success. There is no obvious advantage in making a count of these debts and of acknowledging that list.

But it is absolute protection against pride and thus a strong guardrail against becoming "of the world."

CHAPTER 24

NEVER DISPLAY INGRATITUDE,
EVEN WHEN IT IS DESERVED

NOTHING IS SO DESTRUCTIVE OF YOUR FORTUNE AND your friendships as ingratitude. Especially when it is deserved. When you display ingratitude toward someone who deserves it, the acid of that attitude is delivered in a noncorroding container of justice and will burn forever.

Better to let go or at least keep silent when you ought to turn on someone who—having extended you a minor accommodation—does you a disproportionate disservice.

Imagine that you have made a habit of driving an elderly person to and from a regular appointment. It could be to the grocery store to do the marketing. It could be to a doctor's office for a checkup.

Then imagine after a couple of years of such trips, this acquaintance presents you with a check for a hundred dollars, saying it's time to settle up the gas money.

This should sting a bit; you weren't doing your service for the money. But it would bite deeply if it was accompanied by a note asserting that all along you had been hoping to be so rewarded. At that moment you would be tempted to rise up and speak quite a harsh speech.

This example is a small version of events that play out often in the worlds of business and government. You will have been practicing the rules of previous chapters, striving to build your balance in the favor bank and to assist others in their rising, only to be met with an unexpected and undeserved attack on your efforts or your intentions. You will be stunned. You will be angry. And you will be tempted to strike back.

Don't. Don't ever shake your head in disbelief. There is no upside to showing ingratitude. Even when it is deserved.

CHAPTER 25

STATING YOUR OPINION OF OTHERS

HAVE YOU NOTICED THAT JESUS DID NOT VOICE ANY particularized condemnation of the people of His time on earth, except when He did it face-to-face? Even then it was rare, but find a name of someone Jesus rebuked or talked down out of earshot.

Paul did it: Alexander the coppersmith did him wrong, and he let others know it. And Paul was quick to let others know that Demas was in love with the world. But Jesus didn't do it. Neither, we have to conclude, should we.

But, oh, the temptation! No temptation shall be as universally ubiquitous as the opportunity to trash a rival, a friend, a colleague, a boss, and even underlings when they are not in the room. Such talk is the oxygen of the American workplace. We could scarcely breathe without an occasional gasp of vitriol coming or going in the hallways or near the coffeepot.

I have walked the halls of the West Wing. It thrived there.

I have roamed the corridors of the U.S. Court of Appeals for the District of Columbia Circuit. It was there.

I have sat in the suites of CEOs and COOs, and I have worked in the mail room of Harvard's administrative nerve center. It's in all of those places.

"It" is the desire for advantage advanced through the purposeful diminishment of others' reputations. Even a stalwart anti-Darwinist would have to admit that this very Darwinian behavior is everywhere evidence of a survival-of-the-fittest instinct.

There is not much point in belaboring the obvious. You have trashed your colleagues at least occasionally and perhaps endemically. You have your reasons, and some of them sound good to you. They deserved it. They were destroying the company. They did it first. They obstructed progress. They wouldn't mind. It was funny. It slipped out.

It's a sin in the category of gossip, but my experience is that even the resolutely charitably tongued at home and in church find the challenges of work too much for their resolve.

There are exceptions. Try to think of those folks who are rarely, if ever, heard to denounce others or criticize in a fashion that does not necessarily make its way directly to the target. Exclude those who give criticism and correction directly, eye-to-eye. That's not what we are talking about here. Rather, folks fall into two categories: reputation builders and reputation destroyers.

The former build up their employees, colleagues, and superiors. They are intent on underlining the achievement of others, even when it has no conceivable benefit to themselves.

The destroyers are, of course, the opposite. In their minds, no good reputation ought to stay that way.

Life is a habit of habits, and the habit of trash talk is addictive and destructive. If you've got it, you must break it. If you don't, guard against its appearance.

Christians cannot rise in the world and remain true to their faith if their emerging is even somewhat devoted to the destruction of others in the workplace. They may cause some to fall, but they will slip with them.

Every leader I have served—every one—was a builder of others' reputations. When it was necessary to talk about the failures of others—and I am sure it was necessary—I wasn't in the room.

There are patterns to rising in the world and doing so within a Christian ethic. This is the most obvious of all.

CHAPTER 26

REPETITION IS THE PRECONDITION OF SUCCESS

REPETITION MATTERS IN EVERYTHING. VERY LITTLE IS heard the first time it is said. Very little is learned the first time it is taught. Very little is accomplished the first time it is tried.

I have taught law students for nearly a decade. Because some doctrines are so central to constitutional law, I make a habit of repeating them monthly, giving students a fighting chance of remembering these concepts at exam time and, even more important, when it is time to take a bar exam, the successful passing of which is required to actually practice law.

If you must communicate a message up, down, or sideways, and it is important that the message be received, make a point to repeat it at least a half-dozen times. Leave time in between each repetition for the message to be absorbed and for the recipient to avoid reaching the conclusion that you think he is an idiot.

No one likes to be thought a fool, so spacing between repetitions is essential. But it is better to risk some small amount of peevishness in order to assure that messages are sent and received. Jonathan Swift wrote that it is better to remain silent and be thought a fool than to open your mouth and remove all doubt. It is also better to repeat yourself and be thought a scold than to speak only once and never be heard.

For those involved in raising money—and almost every Christian leader becomes involved in raising money—the key repetition is "thank you." Young Life, the parachurch group in which I invest the most time, money, and effort, teaches all its professional and volunteer staff that every donor must be thanked at least seven times. This simple and powerful advice underscores the importance of both repetition and gratitude. The latter cannot be neglected if the donor is to learn the importance of the gift and his role in the accomplishment of the mission, and the former assures that the gratitude is genuinely communicated.

At the outset of my national radio show on July 10, 2000, I decided to use the platform to bring attention to four particular guests: John McIntyre of RealClearPolitics.com, Assemblyman John Campbell of Orange County, California, Congressman David Dreier of California, and Frank Gaffney, who is president of the Center for Security Policy (www.centerforsecuritypolicy.org). Each individual began to make a weekly scheduled appearance on the program because each deserved, I thought, a national platform and national credibility. Congressman Dreier already had both as chairman of the House Rules Committee, and Frank Gaffney had credibility within the universe of defense and national security experts, but all four set very high standards for their work, and each deserved the repetitions that anyone needs to make an impression on the public.

A regular appearance on my program does not, of course, guarantee a national profile in the way that, say, a regular appearance on Rush's program would. But with an audience in more than fifty markets that is greater in size than the audience of any program on MSNBC and most shows on the other cable networks, those regular appearances are better than, as the saying goes, a sharp stick in the eye.

A second example of the power of repetition: An old friend of mine, Mark Roberts, is a tremendous theologian, professor, and pastor. In early 2002 he published a new book, *After I Believe,* on the details of Christian life. I was pleased for my friend that his book was published, but was startled to find it ranked at 2,317,124 on the Amazon.com book-selling site. I resolved to change this, using the power of the radio program and the surefire technique of repetition. My wonderful audience helped as well.

For one week I opened and closed every segment of my program—there are one hundred segments a week (twenty every day; five each of four hours daily)—with the recommendation that the listening audience purchase Dr. Roberts's book from Amazon.com. Every segment at the open and close—or two hundred commercials backed by my endorsement.

Mark's book rose to number 7, blocked then by Stephen King, who knows a thing or two about repetition.

Mark is a prolific writer, and his second book, *Jesus Revealed,* was published in late August of 2002. Again I took to flagging the book at every opportunity for a week. It began at 1,581,000 and rose to a rank of 10.

On both occasions there was only a good product backed by repetition. Mark's ability as a writer made his books worth reading, but advertising proves again and again that exposure guarantees readers. This is why the most apparently annoying ads repeat again and again. It is hard to break through the noise of the world, so give your message a fighting chance to do so.

CHAPTER 27

KNOW EVERYONE BETWEEN YOUR DOOR AND YOUR DESK

EVERY DAY THAT YOU LEAVE YOUR HOME YOU BEGIN A fairly regular commute. There are small variations, but within a couple of months of settling into a job, you will follow a pretty set path.

Along that path will be faces that will become your acquaintances or remain simply faces.

Recall what C. S. Lewis wrote: "There are no ordinary people. You have never talked to a mere mortal." Each of these faces you pass—the parking garage attendant, the security guard, the cleaning lady, the receptionist—figures in Christ's eternal architecture.

So they should figure in your world as well. You should know them, and more than in just a nodding way. Familiarity comes at many levels, but it begins with a name and a city and perhaps a detail or two about marital status, children, or grandchildren.

Always make a note of the degree of awareness that senior-level managers have of lower-level staff, down to the first rung on the ladder. It tells you a great deal about an individual's heart. If executives or other leaders have a concern for every member of their organization, I believe those leaders are much more likely to be trustworthy on a personal level and dependable in the business world. If their concern goes beyond their organization to those simply in the path of their commute, I am even more inclined to believe in the good character of those men and women.

Beyond this display of trustworthiness, however, is a lesson of Christlikeness in the world. Everyone—even the most repugnant, awful human being—matters to Christ. So, too, must the ordinary folks in our daily paths matter to us. It is quite possible that your entire life's plan has been orchestrated by God to put you in the position to minister to a security guard on the weekend shift, or for that security guard to minister to you. That ministry will not occur if you have never even noticed the guard.

According to the Catholic Encyclopedia, Francis of Assisi believed that courtesy "was the younger sister of charity and one of the qualities of God Himself . . . 'Whoever may come to us,' he writes, 'whether a friend or a foe, a thief or a robber, let him be kindly received.'"

If Francis could extend himself to robbers and thieves, surely the convenience store clerk or the cafeteria aide merits a hello.

· CHAPTER 28 ·

COASTING WILL KILL YOU

I HOST ONE HUNDRED SEGMENTS A WEEK, RANGING from four to twelve minutes in length. That's a lot of time to fill.

Sometimes my producer, Duane, and I will add a regular guest as a weekly feature. At this writing, fourteen of one hundred segments are filled on a regular basis.

While that number might someday go as high as twenty-five, I can't imagine it will ever go higher than that. Pre-programming a week would be too easy. It would quickly go stale. Preprogramming is safe, and it's easy, but it is too close to coasting, to going on autopilot, and it would kill the program within a year.

Just as it will dead-end your career if you allow it to. No matter the calling, there will develop an easy familiarity that repetition brings, and with that familiarity will grow the temptation to enjoy the comfort of the predictable and to allow that pleasure to erode ambition.

You won't fail, but you'll never top out either.

The antidote is obvious. Mix it up. Grab a new assignment. Teach a new course. Talk a new area of expertise. Or if you have to, change jobs or careers.

There are no conveyor belts in the influence hunt. It never comes to you, and you never get there standing in place.

This is classic coach talk, the familiar pattern of phrases and clichés that roll off the tongues of coaches everywhere.

With good reason. It's true.

CHAPTER 29

Always Keep in Mind That Your Work Is Far from the Most Important Work in the World

From April of 1985 to March of 1986, I had the most prestigious business address in the world. The White House.

The address was used even by the few hundred of us who labored in the Old Executive Office Building. If you could eat breakfast and lunch in the White House Mess, then you worked at the White House. I could and did, and it's a heady thing for a twenty-eight-year-old lawyer to be part of the White House Counsel's Office.

I had come to that address from a tour of duty as a special assistant to the attorney general of the United States— another heady experience for a young lawyer, especially after I inherited the Foreign Intelligence Surveillance Court portfolio. This job entailed reviewing all applications for wiretaps on foreign nationals suspected of spying in the U.S. At the height of the cold war the AG was signing off on scores of these applications a week, and my desk was the last stop before his. The court had never turned down a surveillance request, largely because the number of levels of review was so extraordinary.

Because this post at Justice, like the one that followed at the White House, involved access to tightly controlled information, it carried a very distinct sense of privilege that usually accompanies exclusion. The lure of such exclusiveness can be corrupting. (C. S. Lewis contributed a powerful essay on this topic: "The Inner Ring.")

The hierarchy of Washington, D.C., is very developed and usually operates based on proximity to the president—those closest to the president have the most status and carry the greatest air of importance. Permanent Washington, from the editors at the *Washington Post* to the powerful lobbyists along K Street, know that they trade proximity for longevity and are thus a few steps removed from power's center; but they, too, have a hierarchy and a sense of self-importance. So does the permanent bureaucracy and so does the world of the secret agencies. Only in the Pentagon is the hierarchy reasonably clear, and even within the military, organized by rank and seniority, there are subcategories of influence and status.

Each of these organizations has semi-public rules of advancement and penalties for failure. So does every organization, but in D.C. so many media representatives are present and the worldly stakes are so high that the ladders are much more visible to outsiders than with other organizations.

My first two jobs in the D.C. power pyramids were close to the bottom, but they were the bottoms of extraordinarily influential organizations and both jobs allowed me to observe the never-ending Great Scramble.

The Great Scramble has been a fact of life in every capital city of every country in the world in every age of human history. It is the elaborate process by which those who pursue power advance or fall in their quest. Whole books are devoted to Washington's version, and before the ink is dry, they are dated because the force of events quickly elevates or destroys reputations and careers, leveling previously powerful parts or elevating hitherto obscure jobs into overnight pinnacles.

Three observations of D.C. power are as applicable now as they were then, and I believe they apply to organizations outside the federal government.

First, no one is as powerful as he thinks he is. There are always unseen obstacles, new opponents, and sudden shifts in events.

Second, all earthly power fades. Everyone hears this. Most people forget it.

And most important, the most powerful jobs in America may be far less significant than any ministry that provides the context for a conversion from disbelief to belief.

You don't believe that? Then you don't believe the gospel, and you don't believe Christ.

If this book is successful, it will help you prepare for and advance a career that aims at influencing this world. The danger is that as you go about that career, you will forget that influence is a means to an end, not an end in itself, and that by pursuing influence in this world, you have chosen the easier path.

A career aimed at power—even one pursued for all the right reasons and one built on principle and discipline and Scripture—does not involve much suffering. It might and probably will involve setbacks and disappointments, but rarely does an individual seeking influence have to contend with want or physical suffering. Most folks reading this book may at some time or another have to worry about money, but it is the sort of money problem that 95 percent of the world would love to have: How can I afford this new car or that house?

By contrast, most Christians called to full-time ministry will have to sacrifice a great deal, including many creature comforts, in order to be faithful to their calling. The world is so arranged that most important callings are not honored by the world with wealth or status.

But they remain the most important callings because they are involved with infinite arrangements, not mere years or decades.

The most powerful people in history hold the stage for at most fifty years. The revolutionaries of the last century—Lenin, Stalin, Mao—all are almost totally eclipsed already if we measure their influence today. By contrast, C. S. Lewis—a quiet academic and writer of children's books—is everywhere read and still being felt.

But even Lewis's earthly achievements may pale in comparison with the influence of a missionary to a remote tribe who provides the occasion for a single conversion that leads to more conversions, which in turn reverberate through human time.

This is the simple fact of infinity at work.

All of recorded human history—less than five thousand years—isn't even a blink in the time span of the universe. It is even less when measured against God's clock. That vastness overwhelms us, but we have to stay focused on it.

Soul work is about changing the infinite trajectory of a single soul. To assist the Holy Spirit in saving a soul from eternal pain and sending that soul to eternal glory is the most significant achievement any human can aspire to. All other efforts must be judged in relation to their eternal effects, including a life as abundant and significant as Churchill's—easily the most influential man of the twentieth century. Box all of Churchill's tangible achievements—his jobs in a score of cabinets, his books, and especially his triumph, his leadership during WWII—and that box might be nothing compared to the life of a humble missionary who took the gospel to an obscure Amazon tribe. We don't know. We cannot calculate using God's abacus.

(Having written this, I pause to wonder how the church would look today if Churchill had not been there to lead the Allies—if Hitler had not been crushed. Some public figures do God's work by defeating evil's march. In doing so, they give the church breathing room. They, too, are influencing the infinite trajectory. But most of those involved in the Great

Scramble are concerned not with defeating evil, but with defeating their opponents.)

Most nonministry careers are less significant than most ministry careers when evaluated in infinite terms. The time frame of the latter guarantees this. Some are not, of course, but worldly ambition for worldly ends is not particularly significant.

The ability to keep this truth in mind is rare. We forget it every day. We need to remember it every day.

As you go about pursuing success, the best protection of your perspective that you can arrange is an active role in some ministry that is explicitly evangelical. For me, it is Young Life, one of the world's most effective outreaches to adolescents who do not believe in anything, much less God. Young Life's evangelical model is wildly successful, and my work with various components of the organization keeps me always aware of the big battle for souls that is constantly raging, even as my eyes are drawn to the tiny battles between Republicans and Democrats, or even the battles between the Cleveland Browns and the Ravens, the Bengals and the Steelers. Because I go to the meetings of Young Life staff, I am continually reminded that the front line in the world is the line on which people hear the story of Christ and are given the chance to respond to it.

This is a book about earthly power in the service of those engaged in the big battle. Some of us are called to participate in the life of government and culture, but we are at risk of losing sight of the big battle.

Even as you make your plans to advance in the world, make and keep two commitments.

The first, which I will write about later, is membership in a church.

The second is involvement—deep, real, expensive—in a missionary activity. I strongly recommend Young Life (www.younglife.org), but there are many other fine groups like Campus Crusade for Christ (www.ccci.org) and Navigators (www.navigators.org). There are hundreds more.

A lifelong commitment to one of these groups will keep you focused. If you write a monthly check, get a monthly newsletter and, I hope, attend at least a monthly meeting or event, you will be reminded of the big battle and why you are involved in the little battles.

And keep an eye on the obituaries.

The first two rules of the Great Scramble—no one is as powerful as he thinks and all power fades—are harsh realities that catch up with everyone whose entire life is given over to earthly power. I have often come across formerly influential people who are desperate to return to their glory days or deeply embittered by their eclipse.

In 1979, I was twenty-three and working for the exiled Richard Nixon at the old western White House, in San Clemente, California. It was an odd place—the Elba of America—but Nixon was a wonderful boss and a tremendous teacher. The chance to spend many hours a week with him was a tutorial in the reality of power that few ever have.

Some of the lessons had nothing to do with RN, but with the people who came to see him.

As I came out of meetings with RN, I would often pass a visitor. Some were easy to recognize. Woody Hayes and Bill Walton dropped by to see America's Napoleon. So did scores of powerful folks eager to get RN's take on events. (This parade would increase in volume after RN moved to New York in 1980. I left his staff that August for law school, and rejoined it for two years in 1989 to oversee the building of the Nixon Library in Yorba Linda, California. By that time, Nixon's rehabilitation was complete, and his calendar always full of America's A-list of political players.)

On exiting one day, I noticed a man of about seventy wanting to see the president, but I did not recognize him. I asked RN's secretary who he was, and learned that he had been a senior Eisenhower aide in the fifties—one of the bright young men of that era. Thirty years later he was, as I will hopefully be and you as well, a slow-moving, genial fellow in a blue suit whom the young movers and shakers don't recognize. "He used to be quite important," the receptionist explained to me. There are tens of thousands of people in Washington with that tag, and hundreds of thousands more about whom it could be said that they "used to *think* they were important."

The obituaries drive home this point. Almost everyone is diminished by age, and the length of most obituaries of folks aged ninety and above is only a few paragraphs—the world just doesn't care if he was a major filmmaker or she was a gifted novelist. Some folks rank so high that they get a half page in one day's paper, but then the look-back is over, usually forever. Fame always fades.

If you are blessed with talent *and* discipline *and* luck, you may have a pretty good run at the top or near top of your calling. But it will be a run, and it will have an end. That end will likely occur much earlier than your death, and so you will have some years, hopefully many, in which to contemplate your life's work. It is a guarantee that you will be amazed at how quickly it passed. And it is also a guarantee that your investment in your parallel ministry will be at least as important to you as your professional accomplishments. Please do not make the mistake of neglecting this parallel calling even as you pursue the career in the public sphere.

CHAPTER 30

To Repeat: Power Fades

DR. JAMES DOBSON BUILT THE MOST INFLUENTIAL parachurch organization in history. By the time of the twenty-fifth anniversary of Focus on the Family, Dobson's staff exceeded 1,200 people, and his *daily* audience was 220 million spread over 117 countries.

On the occasion of Focus on the Family's silver anniversary, Dobson gave an interview to the *Gazette* of Colorado Springs. Here's what he said:

> Celebrity is an illusion. First of all, it's very temporary, and you can lose it in an afternoon. Secondly, it's not to be taken very seriously. I don't say that falsely humble. I just am keenly aware I'm an ordinary man with ordinary flaws, and some of them pretty pronounced, and I'm just doing the best I can to deal with an awful lot of hurt that's going on out here.

Dobson's musing, along with some reminder of the Great Commission, should be on the desk of every currently powerful leader who is a Christian. The recognition of the fleeting nature of power alongside the primary "must do" for believers should help produce the urgency with which daily work should be attacked.

When James Dobson remarks "you can lose it in an afternoon," he is speaking as a survivor of both heart trouble and a stroke. He knows that he might not make it to the parking lot today, and he acts accordingly. So, too, should you.

When you have the ability to advance the gospel, do so. The combination of power and evangelical purpose is rare, and when these two things intersect, you'll discover a window through which to project the gospel with a unique force and effect.

PART IV

Your Life from 7 p.m. to 8 a.m.

Nothing is as certain as that the vices of leisure are gotten rid of by being busy.

> —Seneca

To be able to fill leisure intelligently is the last product of civilization, and at present very few people have reached this level.

> —Bertrand Russell

The more we do, the more we can do; the more busy we are, the more leisure we have.

> —William Hazlitt

CHAPTER 31

CHOOSE A CHURCH, AND JOIN IT— GENUINELY

I HAVE ALWAYS BELONGED TO A CHURCH. I HAVE belonged to several as I have moved from Ohio to Massachusetts to southern California, then to New York, Michigan, Washington, D.C., Virginia, and back to California.

I occasionally try to count the addresses at which I have received mail. When I get to the number thirty, I give up. But I can count my churches because each has been as distinct as its architecture.

Choosing a church home is not as difficult as choosing a spouse, but it can and often does have as much impact on your life as your mate will. If you take church seriously, it will absorb a large portion of your life and will inevitably shape your weeks, months, and years. A genuine commitment to a congregation of believers is a massive undertaking.

Which is why, of course, so many in America resist the traditional joining of a church. Don't make that mistake.

Every ten years the City University of New York conducts a huge poll of Americans to discover patterns in religious affiliations. When the most recent report arrived in 2002, I got a call from *USA Today*'s reporter Cathy Grossman. She wanted to know what I thought of the marked trend toward switching.

And that is exactly what the data revealed: large numbers of American believers of all sorts had been on the move in the previous decade, leaving old traditions behind and trying on new ones. Catholics had become evangelicals, and evangelicals had become Catholics. Presbyterians departed for orthodoxy, and Baptists headed toward pentecostalism. There was no clear winner or loser in these numbers, just tremendous change.

This is hardly news to pastors who have grown accustomed to one-week wonders and church shoppers. Like the legendary looky-loos of the real estate world, some folks just like visiting churches and don't like joining. So they wander from congregation to congregation in search of the perfect fit.

There is no perfect fit. But you must find a fit, no matter where you live or how often you move. This is a first premise of Christianity. Christ Himself ordained that the church exist and that His followers build it across the globe and through the centuries. There is no exception for the busy young adult on the first few rungs of a career-building plan.

In fact, few people need church more than the recent university graduate, the single man or woman, or the young couple planning on having a family or already having launched one.

Think for a moment about the lessons that will never be taught in school or at work, and the conditions of school or job:

No one is going to give a lecture on service.

No one is going to give a talk on charity.

Few people will offer advice disconnected from personal interest.

The true nature of God will rarely, if ever, enter a conversation.

Ethics may receive some attention, but morals hardly any.

Competition is always present, even when muted.

Pressure to perform will be your constant companion.

And you will almost always be interacting with the same people.

Church is much different. It is everything that work is not. It is a community that is not in competition with you for advancement, salary, or sales.

It is a fellowship where disinterested advice will be plentiful (much of it bad because earnest, well-intentioned people may not understand the circumstances in which you find yourself, or the pressures under which you operate). But rarely will even the bad advice be offered with a hidden agenda.

It is a place where God's role is expressed and Christ's demands should be obvious in spoken and written word.

And instead of earning income there, you will be expected, rightly, to donate there.

If you do not choose a church—thoughtfully and purpose-fully—you are denying yourself a key element to the successful wielding of any influence you will gain.

If for no other reason than the guardrail effect, you should seek out and dive into a local congregation. The guardrail effect is the correcting influence that a community of believers will have on every wrong impulse embedded in young adults. Belong to a church, and you are much less likely to fall into the common sins, and a whole lot less likely to be captured by a deeply destructive character collapse.

Of course, younger men and women in congregations commit all the ordinary sins of the flesh, but not so frequently or with so much abandon as those who are not in congregations. Church is a conscience restorer, of which there are too few in today's culture.

Church can also be a steadying influence on the rush of the career-building years. Things will go wrong. Setbacks will occur. Relationships will smash up, and the best-laid plans will end up in pieces. At those moments your church home will be a refuge—even if no one there is aware of the particular circumstances surrounding you.

And if you choose your church wisely, your faith will deepen as a result—the best benefit of all. Strong church equals stronger faith. It is that simple.

So how to choose? Some rules to follow:

When you move into a community, try to do so with a plan on making a second local move within a short period of time. Try to get a short-term place to lay your head so that you can scout around for a variety of needs, the most important of which is your church. Try to find it before you find your apartment or house. Live close to the church and you'll be at the church more often. Over a year or a number of years, the impact of proximity is huge.

Of course, you have to attend on a trial basis; the preaching and worship style will cement you into the community or drive you away. But give the preacher a chance and listen to at least four sermons. A preacher has good and bad days too.

There is no way to quickly assess the welcoming nature of a church, but a scan of any bulletin will let you know whether there is age-specific ministry. There is a huge advantage to joining a congregation that divides itself along generational lines at least once a week in Sunday school class.

And crucially, though you might not have kids or even a date in the last six months, notice the children's program. The vibrancy of this, often the most thankless ministry, is the best quick read on the life of the church you are assessing.

There are also some warning signs.

Horrible music means horrible music. C. S. Lewis wrote that horrible music was actually a good thing for a Christian to have to endure. Lewis was a genius. But he wasn't always right. Sometimes bad noise is just that and an impediment to worship.

Listen for politics, either Left or Right, from the pulpit. I prefer my pastors to be good moralists and generally quiet on whether unemployment benefits need to run sixteen or twenty weeks. Spare me environmentalism that is a mile wide and an inch deep, and since I do politics for a living, please don't subject me to amateur hour on any related topic. I think you will grow weary of lectures from the Right or the Left, especially if you know a great deal about matters that the pastor does not but he preaches with abandon on them anyway.

Parking will be a nightmare no matter where you attend, so don't count that against the church. And there will be a building campaign, and you will have to contribute to it.

Finally, if there is no missions committee and no sign of the congregation's commitment to the wider world, then the church you are visiting is not faithful to the Great Commission, and it is best to move on. As I write this, my home church has dispatched a dozen volunteers to the Ukraine to help one of that struggling country's newer congregations keep its momentum going, and our members who are resident as Wycliffe translators in Indonesia were welcomed home last week for a few months' stay. Some months I am dizzy with the comings and goings of missionaries. They are giants. Our church does its small part to help them and so should the church you join.

Most of the chapters of this book are encouragements on how to pile up worldly influence for the benefit of the church and Christ. A prerequisite to success in that effort is abandoning yourself to a congregation of God's people. That means making a real commitment of your time and money. You actually have to serve within a community to get the gifts of the church back. It is designed that way.

Although you may hate this paragraph, please believe it: you have to support the church you join with cash, no matter your level of income. There's a huge amount of literature on the benefits of tithing, and it has been proven true over the years that the generous are always the first to declare the benefits of the generosity that have come back to them. I do not mean the gospel of wealth. I have always thought such appeals to be astonishingly bad examples of exposition of Scripture. But I have heard too many testimonies of tremendous spiritual benefits to discard the obvious truth that a generous soul is a happy soul.

And you ought to plunge into a study that is on a day other than Sunday. From such groups comes wisdom as well as life-long friends.

Twenty years ago my wife and I joined a Bethel Bible Study group that formed for a two-year period to complete a well-traveled curriculum familiar to millions of people around the world. We emerged at the end with a better understanding of Scripture, fond memories, and two of the closest friends in our lives with whom we stay in contact often, though separated now by a continent. These are the friendships that cannot be made anywhere outside Christ's community.

Some readers have never experienced such a church, even after years of faithful church attendance. Your family or your congregation may not have been built this way. No matter. You can find and belong to such a community with only minimal effort. Most communities are blessed with a variety of congregations, and the dynamism of the combination of faith and freedom usually means that a new church is being planted somewhere near you.

Whether you have just arrived in a city or town, or whether you have been there for years, look around for the vibrant faith community and go there. Join it. Dive into it. No piece of advice I give is a more valuable than this one.

CHAPTER 32

START AND MAINTAIN A WEB LOG (BLOG)

YOU MAY ALREADY KNOW WHAT A BLOG IS—AN ONLINE diary of your thoughts on whatever crosses your mind. The dominant blog of the day—judging by the number of visitors daily—is Instapundit.com by Tennessee law professor Glenn Reynolds. There are literally thousands more. They represent the most important communications development of the new century. Join the revolution. Start a blog.

You need a Web address and some idea of how to post. This will be second nature for younger people, like telling a fifty-year-old he needs to know how to use a fork. But here's the key: your blog will display you to the world. Understand what that means. Have fun with it, but do not indulge in crudity or viciousness, as other believers will have you thrown back in their faces as an example of Christian hypocrisy.

You can use cutting humor and the other weapons of argument, but be slow to do so because these are not easily mastered and can go very wrong. What you commit to your blog cannot be erased. It will follow you for as long as anyone cares to follow you, and significant people are followed very long indeed, especially by those they injure, whether rightfully or not.

The advantage of blogging is that it will oblige you to live in the world of ideas and debates, and to do so at the modern pace. At present no great blogger has emerged with a distinctly evangelical worldview. When one does, with humor and insight attached as well, that person (or persons) will have an enormous impact on the world.

Begin by studying the key blogs that are currently available, such as Instapundit (www.instapundit.com), the Kausfiles (www.kausfiles.com), the Dynamist (www.vpostrel.com), the Volokh Conspiracy (www.volokh.blogspot.com), and Powerline (www.powerline.blogspot.com). After a few weeks, marry your technological ability to the form, and begin to comment on the world around you. Because blogging is the genuine marketplace of ideas, your site will prosper if you are any good. And so will your reputation—if it deserves to.

CHAPTER 33

FIND INTERESTING PEOPLE

THERE ARE INTERESTING PEOPLE, AND THERE ARE DULL people. Find the former, and seek out as much time with them as possible. Endure with patience the dull people. Recall yet again Lewis's stark warning: "There are no ordinary people." Dull people carry the full weight of God's glory, and they deserve your respect and kindness. If you fail to practice those obligations, your soul will shrivel, and you will lose an essential Christian virtue. Even as the balance of this chapter charts the advantages of time spent with interesting people, keep in mind the Christian's obligations to all people, even the excruciatingly dull.

Interesting people are easy to be with, easy to admire, easy to spot. Many of them are also supremely dangerous to your life in this world and your life in the next. There are plenty of rogues in the ranks of interesting people. Think Bill Clinton. Think Ozzy Osbourne. Indeed, most serial killers are interesting at some level.

There are three classes of relationships within the world of ambition: superiors, equals, and inferiors. Wherever and whenever possible, try to populate each level of relationship in your life with interesting people who are good. Every boss you consider working for, every subordinate you hire, and every alliance you enter into as an equal should preferably be with an interesting, good person.

Interesting is an accordion word that covers an enormous variety of characteristics. It typically includes the tastefully curious, the widely traveled, and the iconoclastically read. You ought to know the three dimensions. Interesting people have many dimensions.

Interesting people will be your teacher in subjects that, as life progresses, you lose the time to master. At twenty-five or even thirty, you will have forfeited the opportunity to do an in-depth study of Chinese history and culture. But there are many, many such experts wandering around America. When one of them crosses your path, make a note and pursue the acquaintance.

A second lesson: when in the presence of an interesting person, do not waste your time on subjects of mutual or passing interest. Within the limit of good taste, always being careful to avoid being overbearing or intrusive, engage the interesting person in his area of expertise. Each conversation is an opportunity to hit the jackpot of insight, so use as many of them as good manners allow.

"Primo Levi, chronicler of the twentieth century's darkest inferno, has been called a Dante for our time." That is the first line in a review of a biography of Levi that appeared in the *New Republic*. Now imagine knowing that line: What would you have done with an hour's conversation with Levi when he was alive? Not talk sports, I hope.

Recently I chanced to share twenty minutes of conversation with a circle of a half-dozen people. One was a missionary—a Wycliffe translator, working on a particular island in the Indonesian archipelago. Within the limits of tact, I hijacked the conversation and peppered the man with questions first about Indonesia and the headlines: Had the Muslim and Christian unrest spread to his island? No. Could it? Possibly, but it was largely confined to a particular region. How had it started? Imported by Al-Qaeda. Had he seen any influx after the start of America's intervention in Afghanistan? Definitely. He had been on a two-day boat trip with many burka-clad women and turban-wearing Arabs and Afghans bound for a safe haven within Muslim communities.

I also got some sense of the nature of the Indonesian jungle and then was treated to an anecdote that will come in very handy if I am ever attacked by a python. My missionary friend has a friend who was unexpectedly attacked by a python in a manner that trapped one arm. The victim used a machete to slit open the snake and pull out the intestines with his teeth (so as not to drop the machete). This was an interesting glimpse into life in Indonesia.

Also of interest was the discovery that Wycliffe translators are given the freedom to choose the order in which they translate Scripture. (Where would you begin, do you suppose?) This information surprised me. I had assumed an organization as venerable as Wycliffe would have long ago deciphered a best practice. But no, the local culture drives so much of the evangelization envelope that the in-country missionary who knows the indigenous people best must make that call on where to begin. (He had begun with Mark and had moved on to Acts. Then he planned Genesis, and from there on to a letter, perhaps 1 Timothy.)

Twenty minutes of talk that might have gone on hours and in many different directions. Expertise was engaged, and the quality of the conversation soared as a result.

If you make a practice of dealing with interesting people in such a way, and if you design your life to assure contact with them, inevitably you will absorb the qualities that make them interesting.

Now the downside.

As I mentioned, interesting people come with characters that can be quite good or bad. The latter have particular appeal.

My longtime producer and great friend Martin loves television assignments that take him to the underbelly of American life. He has covered the crystal meth binges of the streets in Las Vegas and the hypersexual debauchery of South Beach in Miami, Florida. Martin has followed assault-weapon-toting gang bangers in Los Angeles and the drug trade that flourishes on the southwestern border. He produces compelling segments carried on national news magazine programs.

He has also produced most of my God segments, and he loves doing that as well. But God TV is much harder to film because the invisible conflict is just that—invisible. Film at 11:00 of spiritual warfare doesn't come easily, although we found the Harvest Crusade altar call to be quite compelling evidence that the good news can also provide at least occasional good video.

But there is no denying the allure of darkness. Early in my broadcast career I was dispatched to the then very violent center of Compton, California, at midnight to cover the just emerging rave scene. Driving into Compton that night, filming and interviewing the very young participants at the illegal warehouse party, got the adrenaline pumping, as did my drives through the area of the 1992 riot-torn and burning Los Angeles. The rush of violence has captured many in the film and television business, so much so that ordinary charms long ago lost their attraction.

And just like dark and violent events and stories, darker-souled people can be quite alluring. They are magnets for young, not-yet-despoiled adventurers with insufficient time for real adventure and all the libidinous energy of people under thirty-five. Interesting people who are interesting because of what they do at night are best avoided. Period.

And there is my rule of thumb. Very, very little of good occurs after darkness falls. A clear majority, perhaps even a huge majority, of what is bad occurs after sunset. You will live in both daylight and moonlight, but your superiors, inferiors, and equals, chosen for their interesting qualities, are much more likely to improve you and benefit you if the reasons they are interesting—he is the best reporter for the *Post*; she is in charge of programming a start-up cable network—depend upon what they do in the daytime as opposed to how they act under cover of darkness.

CHAPTER 34

AVOID THRILL SEEKING: GENUINE ACCOMPLISHMENTS LAST; ADRENALINE DOESN'T

RICH BOTKIN IS A STOCKBROKER, A RETIRED MARINE officer, and a Hugh Hewitt promoter. Everyone should have a Botkin in his life, for almost daily Rich tracks me down from his office in Sacramento to do an encouragement check, as he calls it. "I love you, man, and I have already prayed for you," his message will say if he gets to the voice mail instead of me. Then he will move on to the column I have written or the broadcast of the day before. Botkin is always on the prowl to motivate and encourage. He's a dynamo, the real deal, and a leader of men. So I asked him while writing this book, which piece of advice he'd like to offer. And this chapter is it.

We live in the age of extreme sports, of ultra-marathoners and parasailors, dirt bikers and triple-loop skateboarders. Folks feel the need to cross oceans in balloons, not for discovery purposes, but for tests of themselves. Bungee jumping and rock climbing, survivor shows and eco-challenges—all of these activities are linked by the need of the participants to feel some sense of thrill, some sense of accomplishment.

And none of it lasts. None of it. The thrill is a fix, and as soon as it is gone, the cycle begins again.

There are genuine accomplishments to be had in the world. Rich is instrumental in supporting Asian Hope, for example, an orphanage in Pnom Penh, Cambodia (www.AsianHope.org). The establishment of this staff and the care of these children are the real deal, a hard-won victory over the despair of postgenocide Cambodia and a lighthouse of faith in a ruined, devastated land. Setting out to help rebuild Cambodia is not a short-term project, and there will be none of the exhilaration of skiing a virgin mountain after having been dropped from a helicopter. But putting brick on brick in Cambodia is an eternal project, not an afternoon's frolic.

Botkin is not a scold, nor am I. We love the outdoors and understand the absolute requirement of seeking simple fun in various pastimes and pursuits. I have run for twenty-five years, and can't imagine not running for as long as the knees hold out. Sometimes, when training for a marathon, for example, I'll spend six or seven hours a week training, but mostly I get in three or four hours a week on the road. This is about what the balanced life requires—an average of a half hour of exercise a day.

But I cannot understand ultra-marathoners or compulsive trainers. I cannot see the advantage of three hours a day in the gym, or every weekend spent scaling rocks. And the whole idea of eco-challenge is just silly navel gazing.

There are serious things to accomplish, and they are set

before each human being. You choose to do them, or you choose to do other things. A love of adventures is a choice to do things for yourself. It is almost always a poor choice that cannot be reversed because of the expenditure of time that is involved. Those who would influence the world cannot afford wasted time. Keep Rich's message in mind. Skip the cliff swinging, and concentrate on the real challenges.

CHAPTER 35

MANAGING YOUR FLAWS

GEORGE W. BUSH DRANK TOO MUCH. HE STOPPED. HE would not have been president had he not stopped. It's that simple.

A high-ranking academic stored pornography on his computer. The porn was discovered when he asked the university to expand the storage of his machine. He was obliged to resign. His flaws crushed his career.

Every successful person you admire has huge flaws—every one. Really. Don't kid yourself about the individual. There are no perfect people; in fact, there aren't even any close-to-perfect people. The folks who rise to the top and stay there for a long time ruthlessly study themselves and bring their flaws under control.

Doing this used to be easier than it is today. Pretty much the only risky vice was booze prior to 1965, and even then the world made room for talented drunks. Powerful men who cheated on their wives could also count on winks and nods.

Even as the American scandal machine destroyed the idea of privacy, so, too, did the temptations grow. The drugs in circulation, the Internet porn industry, the coupling and uncoupling of modern sexual morals added a million more opportunities for misdeeds in the ambitious individual's professional life.

Christians are well acquainted with sin, so this is a short chapter. What a leader of ambition needs to know is that the higher you rise, the greater the target you present, and the easiest way to end a career is to tell yourself that "this one flaw does not really matter." It does and it will.

Younger people seem to believe they get a pass until they are thirty or married, whichever comes first. Some even revel in excess—like the superstars of Enron, renowned for partying harder than anyone else.

This is nonsense and quite stupid. Excess is an indicator of silliness to serious people, and getting hammered is for fools. So, too, is running with the bulls in Pamplona. So, too, is hooking up with strangers.

Most of the free world is managed by disciplined people who rise early and work late, and who take pleasure in their craft. This is an old rule, as old as history. We pay attention to exceptions and tell ourselves that the exceptions are the rule. They are not.

You are quite capable of leaving your vices behind and managing your flaws. More often than not, you best accomplish this by substituting a positive habit for a negative one or cutting off a friend or acquaintance who revels in the very behaviors that are bound to diminish your rise. Entire sections of bookshelves come down to these two admonishments: find new habits and choose better friends.

CHAPTER 36

BE SLOW TO SHOW YOUR KNOWLEDGE

KNOWLEDGE IS A FORM OF POWER, AND LIKE ALL FORMS of power, its display can offend or frighten, just as easily as it can impress or seduce.

Which is why you have to be very careful about putting your knowledge on parade. You can just as easily lose your audience as add to it with ill-timed seminars on subjects about which you are an authority.

"My hour has not yet come," replied Jesus to His mother when she approached Him about the wine shortage at a wedding (John 2:1–10). He relented, and there followed the first miracle. But His restraint, not His use, is the more remarkable aspect of His power.

Two of the early chapters in this book urged that you carefully go about learning certain things—a broad outline of history and at least one subject to an extent that will demonstrate the capacity to learn deeply.

Now the advice is to be slow to show either the broad or the narrow. There is no inconsistency here. Humility is a virtue that is its own reward as well as a very necessary skill.

If you are the sort to write in margins, jot down the names of a couple of braggarts you know. Would you be embarrassed to find your name in some friend's or acquaintance's book? Not necessarily, you should answer, because some people wrongly confuse their inferiority with another's braggadocio. But if your name appeared in the margin of a book posing this question, and the book's owner was an individual you respected, then you would have a problem.

Your learning will be pleasing to someone when it is useful to him or her—either as part of an organization or as entertainment. But even in those settings, knowledge can be threatening in ways you can only dimly imagine. Your competence will contrast with incompetence, and your learning will be compared to another's ignorance.

Recall the dinner party of an earlier chapter, the one in which everyone had to hold forth for five minutes on an area of expertise. Had one of the participants not known anything of the sort to hold the attention and engage the interest of the others, he would have felt embarrassed, and he would have been quite likely to resent the other guests. *What a bunch of blowhard, vain poseurs,* he could have thought, even if it was not true. Men and women are easily hurt, and nothing is more vulnerable than pride.

There are a few ways to deal with this danger, each of which will serve, but one of which is preferable.

First, always ask more questions than you deliver answers

or opinions to. The next chapter deals with this at length, but keep the technique close at hand.

Next, the key difference is between being asked and volunteering your expertise. Even when you are asked for an opinion, there is a danger of going on too long and in too great detail, but restraint is a habit you can develop. No restraint is present when you are busy telling the world how much you know about this or that.

The best discipline against a destructive display of knowledge is a genuine appreciation of how little you really do know. And about this you can be confident: there are hundreds and hundreds of thousands and thousands of people who know vastly more than you do about everything.

A dozen years in journalism have allowed me to interview people from every walk of life. Nuclear genius Edward Teller, the Dalai Lama, historian and at this writing Second Lady of the United States Lynne Cheney, film director Ron Howard, moon walker (and golfer) Alan Shepard, and hundreds and hundreds more have brought into their conversations experiences and insights that I could never have or hope to acquire in a single lifetime's learning.

And people of extraordinary intellect have taught me, whose names you might not know, teachers like Harvey Mansfield and Judith Sklar, Larry Arnn and George MacKinnon.

Throw in many hundreds of hours of conversation with Richard Nixon and the men and women who passed through his office in his retirement, and I have been blessed to see human intellect of the first order at close range and over extended periods of time.

I know a few things, but I know how very little I know. This latter knowledge is an effective brake on pride. I am obliged by my profession to offer opinions on an hourly basis, but I do so with an instant willingness to be proved wrong and to retract wrongheaded conclusions. You are lucky not to have to lay down opinions at such a furious pace or to speak so often on subjects you know little about.

But what about those occasions when you have been served a fat pitch—high and across the middle of the plate? Even then you should think about the effect of swinging from the hips.

First, in a competitive world, you have to consider whether you have been set up. Your enthusiastic embrace of the opportunity to show some feathers could backfire, and might very well have been intended to backfire. Many famous movie scenes are built on the sudden exuberance of an outsider being allowed inside, only to discover that the invitation was a false and cruel one.

But even if the opportunity to display learning or expertise is genuine, you have to assess the effect on your audience. Will your triumph be another's painful defeat? Or will you be wounding the pride of someone who has staked out an opposite position, thereby earning an enemy for life?

"Academic politics are so bitter because the stakes are so

small," Henry Kissinger is famously quoted as saying. Kissinger's insight is applicable far beyond the university. The smallest slights can leave very marked scars, especially when delivered with laughter in the background. It is not the Christian life to wound, embarrass, or play one-upmanship with colleagues, friends, or even opponents, but it's a common vice that anyone can easily fall into.

Expertise is an absolute necessity if you want influence, but it's a dangerous quality and it can lead you into many traps. As it develops, so should humility.

Weight trainers know that muscle groups have to be developed in pairs: biceps and triceps, chest and back, and so on. If one advances too far ahead of the other, injury results.

So are learning and humility paired. We know how to go about the former, and the latter is actually easier to acquire— and not nearly as time consuming.

CHAPTER 37

ASK AT LEAST A HALF-DOZEN
QUESTIONS IN EVERY CONVERSATION

IN THE 1980S AND 1990S, JUDGE WILLIAM WEBSTER filled some very important jobs in the United States. He served as director of the Federal Bureau of Investigation. He then moved to become director of the Central Intelligence Agency. Even in retirement, he became one of the country's roaming "wise men," filling various commission slots and offering various reports.

William Webster was an extraordinary public servant for many years. But he could be quite taciturn. Some would say dull, but *taciturn* is a better word for an individual who held so many secrets.

I had first experienced Judge Webster in 1983. He came to Ann Arbor to address my graduating class of law students. That was five years after I had heard one of the most compelling commencement addresses in the history of commencement addresses, and Judge Webster's talk proved again the essential balance of the universe—for it was an hour-long essay on the exclusionary rule, a rule of evidence of no concern to you and hardly any concern to us. On and on he went, citing cases we had not read and quoting opinions and law reviews that were written to punish audiences.

I had been a speechwriter, and I recognized fairly quickly that this train wreck of an address had been served up by the FBI's communications department. The judge had done a nice thing and accepted a commencement invitation. He asked his staff to come up with some remarks, and perhaps even suggested that it was time to get a bureau position out on the exclusionary rule. Staff went to work and produced a monster, which Webster dutifully read.

The auditorium was full, with about 350 graduating lawyers and their families. It was a warm Michigan afternoon. It was torture. William Webster had made his first impression on me.

About a year and a half later I was a special assistant to the attorney general of the United States, William French Smith. I joined the Department of Justice (DOJ) after a clerkship on the United States Court of Appeals for the District of Columbia with two wonderful judges, Roger Robb and George MacKinnon. I had been helped into DOJ by a speechwriter, Terry Eastland, and by a call from Richard Nixon to Smith's chief of staff, Tex Lazar. I mention this only to underscore a lesson from earlier in the book—entry into the most serious organizations requires both credentials and connections.

AG Smith held a Friday morning meeting of the heads of each division and major agency under his jurisdiction, and that included the FBI. The four special assistants to the AG attended to do various follow-ups, which was typically a great way to spend an hour. The AG would summarize the week just finishing and forecast the week ahead. The table—a huge one that seated at least thirty—would be canvassed for critical developments, then one or another of the heads of departments, divisions, or agencies would give a ten- to fifteen-minute briefing on his or her portfolio.

We were always most entertained when Rex Lee, then solicitor general of the United States, gave a brief on what had happened or was about to happen before the United States Supreme Court. The solicitor general is the country's chief advocate before the nine justices who lay down the final word on the law, and the closely divided court—it has been that way for three decades now—always had key issues moving before it.

Lee always started by saying: "I begin by reminding you that we have to count to five . . ." It was his way of driving home the point that he was not in the business of pushing legal challenges that would be sure losers, even though some of the conservative activists pushed him to do so.

Lee was the best. Judge Webster, very much admired by everyone in the room, was nonetheless the worst entrée on the menu. But he was director of the FBI, and the AG called on him at least monthly. Then a small flashback of the U of M commencement would descend.

Judge Webster was incapable of entertaining talk. It was not in him. He was also quite incapable of small talk. The special assistant with liaison duty to the FBI loved the man but explained again and again that his years as a judge had sealed the small-talk and witty valves shut.

There was no evidence to the contrary. None. Even AG Smith, among the most gracious men I have ever known, seemed to brace himself when Judge Webster rose to give a briefing. Everyone respected Judge Webster, but he lacked flair in the delivery of the spoken word.

All of this leads me to a Christmas party. My wife and I had gone to the Hill for a party given by the special assistant with the FBI duty, Judy Hammerschmidt. Judy and her husband, Hank, were good friends to hundreds, and all of them came to their townhouse for this party.

Washington, D.C. parties swirl as all parties swirl, and people are swept along into groups that form and dissolve. The conversation keeps spinning, and in a successful party there is laughter everywhere.

Deep into this party, as I was chatting with my host and a third person, I looked up and saw to my horror that my wife was talking to Judge Webster. She was alone with him. Indeed, she and the judge were separated from the party flow by a couch. Betsy had gone to look at a painting that Judy and Hank had hung above a mantel, and to her surprise, she was joined in admiration of the work by none other than Judge Webster.

Betsy had survived the Michigan commencement, and she had heard of the judge's briefings. She knew what she was in for.

Half a house away I waited for an appropriate pause in my

conversation to mention to Hank that his painting had certainly caught the attention of an odd couple. When Hank turned, he immediately registered the same conclusion—he needed to mount a recovery effort ASAP. I watched amused as this veteran party giver and goer managed to move across the room without apparent speed while avoiding any but the most fleeting of exchanges until he appeared at Betsy's side. Somehow he guided the pair back to the party's current and the judge to the safety of broader conversational circles.

An exhausted Betsy soon found me, and through much laughter and in a quiet tone, I asked how long she had been in one-on-one conversation with the judge. "About fifteen minutes," she replied. "How did you do it?" I asked. The question was genuine. I found the idea of a fifteen-minute conversation with Judge Webster not involving business to be a sort of Mount Everest of conversation. I still do, even after a dozen years of being paid to ask questions.

"He's a very sweet man," Betsy answered, "and he loves his farm, so I kept asking questions about his farm. I just followed the rule."

Betsy and I had long ago agreed that the most interesting people and the best conversationalists are those who are continually asking questions. These people bring the wood to keep the fire of conversation burning, and they are indispensable to most settings.

Asking questions is not an easy or even intuitive skill for adults. Somewhere between the age of toddling around and the first job we generally learn to go mute in the presence of strangers. Successful people relearn inquisitiveness.

In the space of a quarter hour Betsy guessed that she asked at least as many questions of Judge Webster as there were minutes. She was lucky to have had a father who, upon his retirement from the Marine Corps, bought a grove of citrus and avocado. Colonel Helmer could and did talk a lot about his agricultural adventures, and his daughter had absorbed enough to hold her own in talk about farms.

The judge was a widower, and Betsy knew that, too, so they talked about cooking, normally not a subject that one could safely raise with a gentleman of the judge's age. Betsy recalled that she asked all or nearly all of the questions in the exchange, but that it was pleasant. She admitted that just about the time Hank appeared, she had drawn down her reservoir of subjects since it would not do to ask the FBI director about matters at the office.

I suspect she could have gone on quite longer, skilled conversationalist that she is. The key is to focus on your talking partner and attempt to learn enough about him or her to walk away with an outline of the individual's life.

It is that simple. And 95 percent of folks have never tried it or do not know how to do it.

This skill at inquiry will immediately mark you as different and attractive. Question askers make the weather, and their friends are legion. When you ask a question, you are displaying interest in the person asked—and in most settings this is a great boon to the pride and self-worth of the person being asked. Most people are not queried on many, if any, subjects. Their opinions are not solicited. To ask them is to be remembered fondly as a very interesting and gracious person in your own right.

Once developed, the habit of asking questions will inevitably give you advantages in every setting. You will obviously leave most situations with more information (and friends) than when you arrived, and being an asker allows you control of situations that statement makers rarely achieve. Once you learn how to guide a conversation, you have also learned how to control it. You can express your own opinions as questions, and every human emotion can be conveyed this way.

There are inappropriate questions—coarse, too probing, or simply foolish. I have watched in amazement as some folks offend and offend again with questions about another's income or possessions. Health is a topic best left alone, and there are others. An alert questioner can judge when someone grows uneasy.

But don't stop. Just change directions.

The art of conversation depends upon finding the right vein and then mining it for the benefit of everyone. I listen to conversations for the sure sign of conversational despera-tion—movies—and will usually help out at that moment with a proven lifejacket for any conversationalist in trouble—travel. It is a rare person who will not discuss where he has been and what he has seen, and it is very rare for such talks to be dull. (It is, of course, possible to drive travel into the ground, or to make talk of films inspiring. All rules have their exceptions.)

A few years ago at a church retreat, I was seated with nine other men waiting for lunch and posed one question: "Where is the most beautiful place you have ever seen while on two legs that you could visit again?" (The "two legs" proviso was included to weed out airplane views.) The conversation heated up and the anecdotes flew. A second line of inquiry developed: "Which is the most beautiful city you have seen?" The conversation could have continued for hours and was abandoned only because of the press of a schedule.

Some readers will be frustrated by this point, telling themselves that they get it: let's move on. Few folks realize how poorly equipped for serious conversation they are, and they stay that way because of lack of diligence. But stay with me for a few more paragraphs, so we can talk about the job interview.

Every law school in America hosts recruiters. At some schools the number of representatives from law firms to conduct interviews will reach into the hundreds. Four or more lawyers will arrive and break into teams of one or two, and law students will begin entering offices or cubicles for a ten- or fifteen-minute interview. A firm with two interview rooms can see as many as fifty lawyers in a day. A group of ten or so students will be invited to dinner that night, and then after the interviewers return home and caucus, letters inviting a handful of students to an all-day interview at the firm's offices arrive.

These are the fly-backs that make life at elite law schools so much fun. Firms fly you across the country, put you up at great hotels, and wine and dine you as you explore cities that might become your home. These are the rewards of hard work in hard classes—and of the ability of the student to ask questions. An offer of a job, which follows no less than a dozen and sometimes as many as twenty separate interviews strung back to back during the office visit, depends upon the same thing.

Some poor law students never figure out that the essence of a job interview—the key to the fly-back—is an appropriate display of interest in the firm and, crucially, in the person conducting the interview. It is partially about the student's grades and interests, but it is always about the student's personality. The first two subjects take about a minute to establish, but the scoping of the applicant's personality is the challenge. And it is up to the student to figure out how to put that personality on parade.

The best minds are constantly asking questions and acquiring information. In the legal profession this is the first task, getting the facts. It seems to be the first task in the medical profession as well, as it is in science and many other fields. The best candidates for jobs are thus those asking questions.

Most applicants for all sorts of jobs know this and come equipped with standard inquiries on the business. Most law students ask a boring series of standards that begins with areas of the firm's practice, the life of a young associate, and concludes with the ever-popular inquiry about whether the firm encourages pro bono work.

I have been on the other side of the desk for scores of these interviews as well, and they always amaze me. Every office is an elaborate set of clues to the occupant's life and priorities. There are books on shelves, pictures on desks, framed degrees on walls, not to mention art and the knickknacks that populate most surfaces. Applicants who ignore all this evidence of personality are, to me, doomed to be dull and thus not very interesting to me in the long haul. My partners and I can teach young lawyers how to do many things, but I can't infuse the sort of personality that ultimately makes a successful lawyer. I have rarely voted to hire the lousy conversationalist, not just in a law firm, but in every job setting.

If you are heading into an interview for a job or for any admission or any benefit that you want, the questions will decide your success at least as much as your answers. So practice the questions before you arrive, and keep your eyes open for clues to the passions of the lives of people interviewing you. You are not running the interview, of course, and hijacking it will not sit well with many folks. But you must find an opportunity to explore the life of the person asking the question.

Back to my example of a law student on a fly-back. He will meet with a dozen to two dozen lawyers in fifteen- to thirty-minute increments over one or two days, followed by dinner with many other lawyers. This is an exhausting and very stressful experience that is best managed if the talking part is shared. The applicant has to put the ball in the hands of the interviewers as much as it is in his hands. Period. You have to ask questions, if only to give yourself time to rest and think, but ideally to engage the interviewer.

And that is the key: if you are interested in the interviewer, he will be interested in you.

Always practice for those interviews that will make or unmake your career by developing the questioning skills you will need to make those interviews come alive. Not only will you arrive prepared for the moment you are judged qualified or not for employment, but you will also develop a skill critical to leadership of any organization.

This is a long chapter for such a brief point: ask questions. In every conversation and with every sort of person. And listen carefully to the answers. This practice will set you apart from a vast mass of people too absorbed in themselves to notice the world around them.

CHAPTER 38

THE ESSENCE OF GOOD TASTE IS NEVER TO BE OFFENDED BY BAD TASTE

BEN FRANKLIN WROTE IN HIS AUTOBIOGRAPHY, "HE IS not well bred that cannot bear ill breeding in others." The same sentiment is expressed in this chapter's title, though I cannot find its original author (probably Joseph Epstein or Montaigne, from whom I have been unconsciously stealing for years).

If you rise in the world, you are going to encounter all sorts of people, and many, many of them will be uncouth. They will dress poorly, smell badly, swear profusely, and generally offend you.

And you must never take offense.

It is totally a matter of choice when to be offended—and you make that choice. The Christian ideal is to see beyond exterior manifestations of a life lived in circumstances that did not produce excellent table manners or good grooming habits. There is also enormous self-interest to be served in refusing to turn up a nose or turn down an exchange based on your sensitivities.

Develop the capacity to overlook bad breeding and unfortunate behavior, folks who press you for favors you cannot give and for which they ought not to have asked.

There is a final advantage in this attitude of refusal to be easily offended. If you are amused by shortcomings in manners of others, you will have many occasions for laughter. If, on the other hand, these are opportunities for you to display temper, you are going to be angry a great deal of the time.

Eventually this habit of rejecting offense should mature into genuine graciousness, a quality difficult to describe but wonderful to see. It can perhaps be called welcoming. A gracious host is a welcoming host, and a gracious individual welcomes all comers into his company. The opposite qualities of harshness and condemning attitudes are repellent and nearly never associated with lasting leadership.

There are rare occasions when genuine offense needs to be taken—when a deliberate and malicious insult is given or injury intended to you, your family, or your friends. But these are rare, rare occasions. When they arise, anger, not dismissiveness, is called for.

Graciousness is a very subtle quality, not likely to be remembered after a brief encounter. But those who practice it and infuse it into their entire lives will find it is the quality of their lives most remarked upon by those with whom they have worked or played.

CHAPTER 39

PRACTICE FLATTERY AND ENCOURAGEMENT

FLATTERY HAS GOTTEN A BAD REPUTATION. SINCERE flattery is simply a subset of encouragement, a noble and good practice. We need to practice encouragement and not run from it because it has sometimes and in some places been used by insincere people.

Flattery is a common denominator of the careers of successful people. There is no denying this. Had the videotape of every successful person's early career been lodged on permanent collection status, we would be able to rewind and replay every past rise and isolate those moments when flattery was put into the service of ambition.

But there is no shame in genuine flattery. In false flattery are deceit and eventually a soul-destroying dishonesty. So here is another edge on which the ambitious have to work: When to use flattery? And when to resist the easy advance it can bring?

Flattery is simply praise or encouragement by an underling. Praise from an equal or a superior is just that—praise. It carries no significance other than the acknowledgment of merit, which can be quite satisfactory if you are on the receiving end.

But flattery always *ascends*. It is directed *up*. To a boss. To a leader. To someone in a position to help.

So flattery always arrives devalued. The recipient cannot help noticing the origin. No one dislikes genuine appreciation and encouragement. But flattery almost always carries the risk of appearing insincere.

Many writers have warned political leaders about flatterers. They are not to be trusted. But how they can seduce!

The proper use of flattery may be one of the three or four crucial ingredients to rising. Some can rise on the force of talent alone. But like the tree falling in the forest that no one hears, talent that is unobserved is not talent at all. Talent requires recognition. Flattery can be the fuse of recognition. There are others, discussed in other places. But flattery pays. So pay attention to it.

Here are the rules:

1. No one underestimates his genuine worth. Some can overestimate their contributions to whatever endeavor is succeeding. But whether the subject is family, business, club, or church, no one underestimates his value to those organizations. (Those who judge their contributions to be worthless fall into two categories: those who are speaking the truth, and those who know that this declamation is not true, but who make it because it's pretty effective as an attention-getting strategy.)

2. All people enjoy recognition of their worth. I've never known anyone who didn't. Perhaps such a person exists for whom justice is repugnant, but the matching of talent to recognition is a natural harmony and should be enjoyable.

It's a wonderful thing, for example, for the long-ignored guard on the offensive line to have his name called during a film session and praised as the key to the seventy-yard breaking run leading to a touchdown. And the secretary who is really the organization's aorta may not need recognition of her service, but it surely is pleasant to receive.

3. Because people never underestimate their worth, they can be assumed to know a rough higher limit of their worth as well. Many folks may overshoot the mark but not by gross factors. (Again, this is within an individual's conscience; public bluster is an altogether different matter.) Because everyone has a rough idea of the higher limit of worth, excessive praise directed up a chain of hierarchy will brand the giver as a brownnoser—a liar, in other words.

So praise directed north carries a risk. But the right amount of flattery carries a reward, and it is also good for the soul.

4. It is a good thing to develop a habit of just judgment. Leaders must exercise just judgment, or they will not be effective leaders.

Take the military. If senior officers cannot accurately evaluate junior officers, incompetent officers will rise—a troubling thought for us all. Though the danger is easier to see in a military hierarchy, the same problem is true in all settings.

The CEO who cannot judge and promote talent will destroy a corporation in short order.

So with these four rules in mind, here is the guide to flattery: when you are genuinely impressed by a superior's leadership, tell him. Do so when you are alone, or in writing; do so with precision and do not linger. But do it.

Do not do it often, however, even if you are often impressed. Give flattery a big rest after every use.

For all other relationships—those of equals and inferiors—never stop praising and encouraging. Every day. All day. Encouragement and praise cost nothing and give huge value when deserved.

Conduct a quick test: write down on this page the people whom you have encouraged this week. Really encouraged. You should be able to recall those instances immediately. If you can't or the list is not long, you are not on the leadership track.

CHAPTER 40

Your Shape Will Shape
Your Success

Some people will be disheartened by this chapter. They have not been blessed with a metabolism that burns calories like a furnace, they never developed the discipline to fight back against nature, or their efforts didn't work. They are out of shape, and it costs them.

This is a hard reality. God doesn't much care what you look like, though He is not neutral on the sins of gluttony or drunkenness. But the world cares. Very much. If you are a slob, the book you hold cannot help you. Really, it can't.

There are a few exceptions to this rule, but very few. The world prizes discipline, and weight problems betray a lack of discipline. In all but a few cases, overweight people receive very little slack from those who can help a career.

Understand this from the point of view of the mentor. If the individual to whom you turn for help on the way to power is judged by anyone on the quality of the people he mentors, he cannot be in a hurry to be seen as an advocate of the undisciplined.

Change the way you look if the way you look is an obstacle. This isn't a diet and exercise book, and truth be told, you don't need one. Exercise more. Eat less. Walk, then run, every day. Every day. It is a lifesaving and career-enhancing habit of the highest order.

And though I find it astonishing to have to say this, I tell my law students every year: if you dress like a bum, people will think you are a bum. They won't give you a pass for being an iconoclast or points for being an individualist. You will be tagged as odd at best or very strange at worst. With clothes, as with all grooming, the ambitious are best served by the very traditional virtues of cleanliness and modesty, and by a shopping habit that seeks classic clothes. This utterly staid advice and your reaction to it will tell you volumes about your seriousness. If it strikes you as hilariously retro, then you value making an impression with other than your talent. If, on the other hand, this is the most obvious of advice, you are on the right road.

CHAPTER 41

SOME MORE THOUGHTS ON MONEY

I REPEAT AND EMPHASIZE WHAT I SAID EARLIER: NEVER carry credit card balances longer than a month. If you have to, you are not managing your finances well, and they will eventually disable you. Buy only cars and houses on time.

Consumption is a constant in America. We are always buying things. Shopping is a part-time job, and marketing is a science. There is nothing wrong with this, although shopping or consumption has never been associated with serious people.

When Philippine's First Lady Imelda Marcos fell from power and her closets revealed thousands and thousands of pairs of shoes, she set a standard for obscene consumption. Her example is a good one for most people to study. Buying too much and displaying it, too, will obviously lead people to conclude that you are flawed.

So don't. Indulge only in a few books, an excellent car, or a fine stereo. But if you must have the best of everything and everything must be new, then you are not serious about rising in the world.

You may already be in a hole. If you are, seek counsel with some gray heads about getting you out, and don't get in deeper. Sell the house you cannot afford, for example, or unload the car payments that are making you borrow more monthly. Don't wait for the big break or the inheritance. Change the way you spend money, and concentrate on how to save it. As you learn to save wealth, you will also be saving your ambitions.

Brian Hampton, my editor, read this chapter and wrote a query about why I was revisiting the subject of money, and why I was doing it in such a brief way.

Simply put: this is where many, many young people screw up. Our culture teaches young people to consume and to always want more. It is the first time in human history when people have spent all their lives being conditioned to buying as opposed to saving. The effects on all lives can be devastating, but especially so on the life of an ambitious young man or woman.

CHAPTER 42

There Is No Advantage in Trash Talk

STANDING IN LINE AT THE SECURITY CHECKPOINT LINE at Denver's airport, I was treated to an extensive conversation between two colleagues concerning the shortcomings of a third colleague—not present, of course. The individual being discussed promised raises he knew he couldn't deliver, was cheap on the road, and was a friendless, Peter Principle–displaying, rotten guy.

Very interesting and very amusing, but of zero usefulness to either participant unless, in the great scheme of things, the missing colleague eventually befriends one of the two. Then the other from the airport has cause to wonder when his negative assessment of the missing colleague will be relayed to him.

A rule I tell my law students and my radio colleagues: there is never any upside in critical comments about anyone made to anyone not in a position to correct or admonish the target of your criticism. Even when you are communicating with a superior about an inferior, carping or critical comments diminish the speaker.

Again and again I hear negative comments made in idle chatter. I always make a note to myself that the speaker is reckless.

Everything said can be repeated and usually is. Everything left on voice mail can be played for audiences of millions. Every e-mail you send can be forwarded to long, long lists, either voluntarily or not.

Scripture is explicit about the evil of gossip and hurtful speech, and the habit of trash talking can become deeply ingrained in folks unused to making serious conversation. The wrongful chatter will also diminish your career.

There is virtue in being closemouthed, and a great reputation in the saying that this person or that person is discreet.

Discretion is all about judgment, about trustworthiness. A reputation for discretion is not easily earned, but it is pretty easily forfeited, usually by a willingness to quickly diminish the capabilities of colleagues or to pass along shared assessments of others.

One last attempt to drive this home: whenever you diminish another to a third party, you are trusting that third party to never repeat the estimate, or to do so accurately and with all appropriate context. If you list a half-dozen qualities about your colleague down the hall, and five of them are glowing descriptions of his industry, thoroughness, good cheer, team approach, and selflessness, and you add that you'd never know it because his office appears to have been hit by a tornado, expect that your conversation partner, in a week or two, will meet your colleague for the first time and say, "Oh, Joe told me about you. You're the guy with a pigsty for an office."

It happens. Every day. So resist the temptation to prepare extensive or even trivial charts of others' shortcomings.

CHAPTER 43

CONFLICT IS PART OF THE CHRISTIAN LIFE

DO NOT THINK THAT I CAME TO BRING PEACE on earth. I did not come to bring peace but a sword. For I have come to "set a man against his father, a daughter against her mother, and a daughter-in-law against her mother-in-law"; and "a man's enemies will be those of his own household." He who loves father or mother more than Me is not worthy of Me. And he who loves son or daughter more than Me is not worthy of Me. And he who does not take his cross and follow after Me is not worthy of Me. He who finds his life will lose it, and he who loses his life for My sake will find it.

—Matthew 10:34–39

Somewhere in the past generation, Christ was hijacked by the pacifists who have attempted to turn Him and thus His followers into New Age mystics, speaking platitudes about universal love and peace on earth. Jesus was very much the perfect example of love and forgiveness, but He was as blunt as anyone in the world, as clear as anyone in history, and uncompromising on the key issues. These attributes make His declaration cited at the beginning of this chapter quite understandable, though the pacifist clique has agonized over it for years.

At this point you may be thinking about Jesus' command to turn the other cheek, and other greatest hits from the pacifist's gospel. Keep in mind: there is a personal gospel and a collective gospel; a gospel of how we are to bear injuries to ourselves and one of how we are to react to injustice done to others. The cheek must be turned when injuries are done solely to you. But conflict has to follow whenever evil is done to the innocent.

In the United States we are blessed with the right to combat evil peaceably, with votes and donations. But abroad this is not the case, and in history such countries have been rare. We are obliged to fight political battles at home and to support just wars abroad. Christians who abandon the innocent to the evil forces in the world are abandoning Christ's instructions.

It is the Christian's duty never to raise the level of conflict unnecessarily, or to make himself a law unto himself. But uncomfortable or dangerous undertakings—say, a war with Saddam's Iraq or whichever nation or tyrant threatens the world in the future—cannot be wished away or taken off the table by a selective theology.

Keep Matthew 10 handy, for in the life lived in or around power you will often hear the pacifist criticism. Understand that criticism is sophistry.

· CHAPTER 44 ·

CHRISTIANS ANGER ONLY RARELY AND ONLY RIGHTEOUSLY

ANGRY CHRISTIANS LIKE TO POINT TO CHRIST'S clearing the temple of money changers. If Jesus could flare and excoriate, surely His followers will as well.

To which wise people respond that you need the wisdom of Christ to know how to act like Christ, and His episode of anger is devastated in number by His episodes of charity. This argument suggests that a believer is much better off staying far from anger because its display is such a rare thing, not just in the Gospels, but also in Acts and the letters.

Anyone aspiring to influence is going to run into anger again and again. Politics, for example, is really controlled mental combat, and like the real thing, mental combat brings forward anger on a regular basis.

To engage in public policy means to engage in fights, and fights produce anger. To duel with opponents inside or outside government is to find yourself in conflict, and conflict breeds anger. Even office politics can erupt, often without much warning.

For a dozen years of law practice, I have been obliged to deal with maddeningly officious petty tyrants of the U.S. Fish and Wildlife Service and some of their colleagues in other agencies. Because many of these individuals view their "mission" as superior to the rights of landowners, and often deem it superior even to the letter of the law, they have operated without regard to the rule of law and with a brazen willingness to break rules, deals, and words when they felt moved. As most everyone who deals with the Endangered Species Act will tell you, it is the harshest law when it comes to law-abiding citizens; it divests them of use of their land, without any payment, and it is administered by an agency full of incompetent, arrogant, and venomous ideologues. The good folks in the agency, and there are many, are outnumbered.

As you might suspect, this agency can and has produced regular eruptions of anger in me and almost all other skilled lawyers who know how it ought to be and realize just how out of control and imperious the agency has become. Add to this my years in the federal government, especially my years as general counsel and deputy director of the federal agency charged with administering the federal civil service, and my anger can be volcanic. I know how those officials are supposed to act, and I know how the law they administer is supposed to be administered. Their indifference to the law and to the citizens they are supposed to serve outrages me.

I am obliged to use anger to make points and to get the attention of bureaucrats used to smug superiority. In other words, anger is a tactic that, to be effective, must be genuine and controlled. Nothing is less effective than perpetual anger; anger can have amazing and rapid effects if it is used appropriately—but only if it is justified.

Bill Clinton was famous for his rages, so much so that their predictability undermined any purpose he might have had. He developed a reputation for petulance, which has little to do with righteous anger.

The younger you are, the less entitled you are to anger. Angry young people simply appear to be arrogant. It is almost always self-defeating to give in to or attempt to use anger before you are thirty-five.

Similarly, anger in older people is easily dismissed as crotchety orneriness.

But it is a powerful tactic in a fully developed leader who knows what he's doing. It is rarely seen in public for a reason, and when it is seen, it is a marker of high stakes and lasting impressions.

In the middle of a debate between candidates for the presidency that had been organized by his campaign, Ronald Reagan once famously announced, "I paid for that microphone." He showed a flash of anger that contrasted with his geniality. That is the perfect contradiction: a reputation for good humor and a ready laugh are the frame in which flashing anger is always best displayed. Don't bother with the anger until you have built the frame.

Time and again listeners compliment me on my patience

with callers with whom I disagree, who are nervous, or who are quite obviously foolish. But almost every listener who has heard me blow up on air—memorably, with a self-proclaimed doctor who repeatedly asserted that American forces killed twenty-thousand civilians in Afghanistan, a libel of huge proportions that I would not let pass—remembers the exchange vividly and understands its significance as well. Listeners understand the essence of the show and of me when they recall the occasion of anger. I try to keep in mind that if I am easily and often angered (as is the case with some in politics and in the broadcasting world), it would quickly become a carnival trick.

As it is with me, it is with everyone. Better never to display anger than to display it too often. Ask your friends and spouse: "Do you recall any occasions on which I was really angry?" If everyone has a story or two to tell, and all the stories are different, you have overplayed anger and have a problem that needs correcting.

But if no one can recall your ever being angry, ask yourself whether you are really engaged in any pursuit to which you are passionately committed.

CHAPTER 45

MARK AND CONTINUALLY REVIEW THE LIMITS YOU WILL NOT TRESPASS

AMBITION IN MOST PEOPLE WILL RESPECT THE boundaries established by the law. Most people will not rob or steal to advance their goals, or commit fraud upon customers or employees. Despite all the headlines of the past few years, the vast majority of businesspeople do not loot their companies or swindle their shareholders.

And the vast majority of lawyers do not lie, nor doctors cheat, nor police beat handcuffed suspects. Media will focus on the exceptions to these general rules, but they are general rules. Most people limit their ambition rather than risk the punishments that accompany going past the limit of the law.

Christian ambition is at a disadvantage, however, because it is limited by a much more extensive set of restraints. Most of these trace a pedigree to the Ten Commandments, but others are more radical still.

Some of these restraints oblige Christians to set aside very effective tools for advancing careers and agendas. Two are extremely useful to both, but are off-limits not because of the law, but because of the faith: cruelty and revenge.

The desire for revenge is among the most powerful that people who aim high will find themselves dealing with. One of the great names of ancient Rome, Sulla, went so far as to inscribe his tomb with a message concerning revenge: "No friend has done me a favor, nor enemy an injury, that I have not repaid in full." More recently the Kennedy family is attributed the maxim that "revenge is a dish best served cold." When people aim to achieve significant things, they take the names and numbers of those who get in their way. Christians can take the same names and numbers—not for the purpose of revenge, but at best for avoidance or maneuver. If you find yourself gleefully keeping a list and telling yourself that "paybacks are hell," you are far off the road and not made of the right stuff for a great calling.

Worse still than the desire for revenge is an inclination to cruelty. This is the clearest marker of diseased ambition. Cruelty can manifest itself in hundreds of ways, from cutting humor to vicious words, from physical violence to emotional abuse. Leaders and other powerful people throughout history have embraced cruelty, often in the name of Christ and to the shame of His church.

Author and journalist Robert Kaplan wrote a book in 2001, *Warrior Politics,* in which he brought together a number of the teachings on ambition and leadership from outside Christian history. Among the stars of this sky is Machiavelli:

"Machiavelli believed that because Christianity glorified the meek, it allowed the world to be dominated by the wicked: he preferred a pagan ethic that elevated self-preservation over the Christian ethic of sacrifice, which he considered hypocritical." Kaplan's summary of the philosophy of the author of *The Prince* is excellent but he takes great pains to rehabilitate Machiavelli by noting examples from American history of leaders using harsh tactics. "Lincoln," Kaplan wrote, "was sufficiently ruthless to target the farms, homes, and factories of Southern civilians in the latter phase of the Civil War." To this observation could be added Truman's decision to use atomic weapons in Japan or any harsh measure from America's long catalog of necessary and just wars.

Machiavelli's signature maxim—"It is better to be feared than loved"—simply cannot be reconciled with a Christian approach to power, however, and the popularization in recent years of books like Kaplan's or the original texts on seeking power from Machiavelli or Sun-Tzu or the like (even when read seriously and not collected for show on desks in Hollywood, where pretenders every day think of themselves as "warriors") is dangerous. The Christian seeks influence for the particular reasons laid out earlier, and the embrace of the pagan ethic endangers the ends of Christian ambition. Cruelty and the thirst for revenge, especially, will disfigure even the highest calling in pretty quick order.

Which is why a rolling inventory of your ambition is called for. Catholics know the old discipline of confession could easily degenerate into a rote recitation of sin, but the sacrament was designed to trigger a genuine examination of the conscience. Protestants, too, are often exhorted to examine their failings and seek forgiveness, but in the course of the average worship service, this has become a five-minute segment, perhaps the only five minutes a week in which the ordinary Christian looks with a critical eye on his or her shortcomings.

The rote sort of examination will not do for anyone of even small ambition, and will fail completely if ambition soars. The opportunity to go "Machiavellian" is always present when power and influence are around. The guardrails become fewer and lower as authority increases. The habit of genuine examination is thus the spiritual discipline most necessary to people of ambition. And the best place to start is with the occasions of cruelty and the desire for revenge. If either or both are in your mind or in your past, and you do not regret the cruelty or still nurse the desire for revenge, you are better advised to give up the ambition that led you to them. "For what will it profit a man if he gains the whole world, and loses his own soul?" (Mark 8:36).

CHAPTER 46

KEEP ONLY THE IMPORTANT STUFF: CLUTTER IS AN ANCHOR ON AMBITION

INEVITABLY THE MOST SUCCESSFUL PEOPLE ARE WELL organized. This doesn't mean having a clean desk or even a good idea of where you left things lying around. Rather, it means a clear understanding of what is important and what is not, and an appropriate allocation of time for each.

One of the most important habits you will develop is the decision to record only important data. There is a ton of data in everyone's file, and e-mail is causing this monster of data to grow and grow and grow. Develop ruthlessness about this. Don't respond to silly, uninvited e-mails. Don't keep business cards you won't use. Don't return phone calls from cold callers.

But hoard the information that could matter, and whenever possible, speak it to someone else as a means of memorization.

If your boss or client enjoys skiing in Aspen, explain that to your friend or spouse, and try to accumulate a little additional knowledge on Aspen or surrounding regions. If your counterpart in a different agency is reading a particular book on Iraq, don't try reading that book, but scan its listing and its reviews at Amazon.com. Not only do such exercises commit your colleague's habit to memory and equip you well for your next meeting, but you also pick up a small dose of Iraq-specific knowledge and you are training your mind to observe the key elements of others' lives.

This habit of information acquisition and retention defines all the great leaders I have met. There is not one exception to this rule. They remember people and their lives, and they connect as a result of it.

It is not an accident, but a habit, among the easiest to acquire and perfect.

CHAPTER 47

To Repeat: Be Slow to Be Offended

PORTIONS OF THE BOOKS I HAVE RECOMMENDED IN these chapters contain detailed descriptions of violent, blood-soaked battles and graphic accounts of a variety of sexual encounters. Either or both will shock a lot of readers. Some of the advice I have given—such as the necessity of choosing between being a pastor or a politician—is guaranteed to offend some.

Leadership is not for the easily offended. The world is full of sex, violence, greed, filth, grime, and rotten people. Good accounts of the world will be full of the same, and your life will be as well.

If you are the sort to proclaim, "Why, I never . . . ," then I hope this book has hit you between the eyes. If you spent a lot of time worrying over whether Harry Potter would induce children to practice sorcery, we are not on the same page, and we aren't likely to ever get there. The Potter books are wonderful stories of good versus evil. Period. Just like *Star Wars*. Just like the *Wizard of Oz*. Just like Narnia. Myths intended to explain truths to us. As I watched the small storm of outrage explode over Potter, I again saw a measure of the Christian distance from the world.

Ancient Greece and imperial Rome were places and times of huge excess. So is our time. If you are the sensitive sort, this is not a book for you, and your calling to leadership needs explanation. You are choosing to be out of the world.

Jesus was not easily offended. In fact, I think He was offended only by the desecration of His Father's house. Keep that in mind.

Christians know that taking offense displays a sense of moral superiority, an objectively impossible status, given the gospel. Your mission in life may be to reduce or end objectionable behaviors and conduct that give offense to others, but sensitivity is not a luxury the world allows its leaders.

Why write a second chapter on a theme so closely related to that of Chapter 38, "The Essence of Good Taste Is Never to Be Offended by Bad Taste"? Because many careers are derailed by hypersensitivity. Very successful people have little time for those with long lists of grievances, real or imagined, but especially those that are imagined.

So if your feelings are hurt but you are not bleeding, get over it and get on with it.

PART V

AT THE END OF YOUR LIFE

THEY CAME TO JERUSALEM. THEN JESUS WENT INTO THE temple and began to drive out those who bought and sold in the temple, and overturned the tables of the money changers and the seats of those who sold doves. And He would not allow anyone to carry wares through the temple. Then He taught, saying to them: "Is it not written, 'My house will be called a house of prayer for all nations'? But you have made it a 'den of thieves.'" And the scribes and chief priests heard it and sought how they might destroy Him; for they feared Him, because all the people were astonished at His teaching. When evening had come, He went out of the city. Now in the morning, as they passed by, they saw the fig tree dried up from the roots. And Peter, remembering, said to Him, "Rabbi, look! The fig tree which You cursed has withered away." So Jesus answered and said to them, "Have faith in God. For assuredly, I say to you, whoever says to this mountain, 'Be removed and be cast into the sea,' and does not doubt in his heart, but believes that those things he says will be done, he will have whatever he says. Therefore I say to you, whatever things you ask when you pray, believe that you receive them, and you will have them. And whenever you stand praying, if you have anything against anyone, forgive him, that your Father in heaven may also forgive you your trespasses. But if you do not forgive, neither will your Father in heaven forgive your trespasses."

—Mark 11:15–26

CHAPTER 48

THE OBLIGATIONS OF A BELIEVER

As I was putting the finishing touches on this manuscript in August 2002, the *New York Times Review of Books* carried a witty article on the outpouring of "how to write novels" books. The author, Dwight Garner, had some fun with himself—a frustrated novelist—and with the authors of "the load of self-help books for would-be fiction writers." "What is it about these how-to-write books," wondered Garner, "that makes even sane people sound like addled swamis?"

There's a warning for anyone offering advice to anyone on anything. Beware sounding like a swami! I hope to have avoided that pitfall, but there is no avoiding its twin—the restatement of the obvious. The very best how-to books are extended restatements of the obvious. No one ever complains about assembly directions that are too detailed and too clear, and no collection of ideas on how to achieve anything should overlook the great and good advantages of pounding home the most obvious lessons, especially when a large part of the intended audience is relatively young.

So I close with yet another restatement.

The world is in trouble, and it needs your help. The church is in trouble, and it needs your help. Christ cared deeply for the world and His church, and indeed, for every single soul within His creation. He did not give any of His believers a pass on the work of the world; He called them into it.

Some people have the talent to change the direction of the world. Some have the talent to change the direction of the church. All of us have the abilities to change the directions of individual lives.

And we are accountable to do so.

The keys to influencing the world are discipline, persistence, and patience. The key to influencing the world in the right way is the gospel.

If you are one of those people endowed by God with a set of talents that will allow you to accumulate influence in the world and eventually power, you ought to set about that business now. Plant yourself in a church, and hedge yourself with close friends who can keep you anchored when the particular dangers of living in the world come close, but do not allow yourself the easy way out—of easy volunteer work or a life of prayer for the world but no action.

Christians are called to defend the church, and that means politics. That means voting and campaigning and contributing—at a minimum. A politically inactive Christian in the United States is turning his or her back on the church in the world, especially its most persecuted parts. This uncomfortable fact obliges you to get involved in the often repellent work of politics. You may find it distasteful, or you may love it. Your personal feelings about politics really don't matter. Having been blessed with this gift of freedom, you cannot bury it and hope Christ doesn't care that you did nothing with the talent He gave you.

So please consider that your place in the world, your abilities to influence it, to participate in politics, to help leadership, to raise money, to organize activity, are exactly like the talents entrusted to the servants in the famous parable of the talents from the gospel of Luke:

> He spoke another parable, because He was near Jerusalem and because they thought the kingdom of God would appear immediately. Therefore He said: "A nobleman went into a far country to receive for himself a kingdom and to return. So he called ten of his servants, delivered to them ten minas, and said to them, 'Do business till I come.' But his citizens hated him, and sent a delegation after him, saying, 'We will not have this man to reign over us.' And so it was that when he returned, having received the kingdom, he then commanded these servants, to whom he had given the money, to be called to him, that he might know how much every man had gained by trading. Then came the first, saying, 'Master, your mina has earned ten minas.' And he said to him, 'Well done, good servant; because you have been faithful in a very little, have authority over ten cities.' And the second came, saying,

'Master, your mina has earned five minas.' Likewise he said to him, 'You also be over five cities.' Then another came, saying, 'Master, here is your mina, which I have kept put away in a handkerchief. For I feared you, because you are an austere man. You collect what you did not deposit, and reap what you did not sow.' And he said to him, 'Out of your own mouth I will judge you, you wicked servant. You knew that I was an austere man, collecting what I did not deposit and reaping what I did not sow. Why then did you not put my money in the bank, that at my coming I might have collected it with interest?' And he said to those who stood by, 'Take the mina from him, and give it him who has ten minas.' (But they said to him, 'Master, he has ten minas.') 'For I say to you, that to everyone who has will be given; and from him who does not have, even what he has will be taken away from him. But bring here those enemies of mine, who did not want me to reign over them, and slay them before me.'" (19:11–27)

Every ability you have—and the sum of those abilities—gives you opportunities to influence the world. And this is a crucial point: Christ does not consider these opportunities to be optional. He has clearly said that they are obligations.

Treat them as such.

ACKNOWLEDGMENTS

SEALY AND CURTIS YATES ARE BEHIND HUNDREDS OF books, and their influence in the world is quite extraordinary as a result. They are models for the sort of career I am writing about. More than agents and lawyers, they are teachers and friends and finders of the good.

Mike Hyatt, executive vice president, and Brian Hampton, vice president and editor in chief, at Thomas Nelson teamed with Sealy and Curtis to bring me out of writing retirement. Kyle Olund provided a practiced eye as well to the editing. Broadcasting is much easier than writing, so I appreciate the encouragement and confidence of these folks in this project.

Ed Atsinger and Stu Epperson are changing broadcasting for the better. They provide me a platform on which to work at Salem Communications, and I am grateful for that opportunity. They are also models of what it means to be fully committed Christians at work in the world.

Russ Hauth brought me into the Salem broadcasting family and encourages my work there on a weekly basis. The

Salem team includes many extraordinary people: Duane Patterson, Anthony Ochoa, Adam Ramsey, Jennie O'Hagan, Clint Redwine, Russ Shubin, David Spady, Greg Anderson, just to name a few. I thank them all.

This manuscript, like all my others, has been meticulously proofed by Snow Philip and overseen by the wonderful Lynne Chapman, my assistant for more than a dozen years. Richard Botkin is a motivator without parallel, and Lynne and I thank him.

Dean Parham Williams and my colleagues at Chapman University School of Law support research and writing outside the ordinary channels of legal research. It is a wonderful institution with which to be associated, and my special thanks go to John Eastman and Tony Arnold, two colleagues who are very generous with their time and insight on all subjects.

Kirk Winslow and Ryan Nielsen provided crucial insight on some of the theological issues covered in the book, and Graham Forrester has been a wonderful research assistant. All are young pastors of extraordinary promise, and I thank them.

My wife Betsy is the best gift God has given me and the full explanation of every good thing I do.

ABOUT THE AUTHOR

HUGH HEWITT is the host of *The Hugh Hewitt Show,* a nationally syndicated radio talk show and a professor of law at Chapman University School of Law. He is a graduate of Harvard College and the University of Michigan Law School. Hugh is the author of three previous books, one of which was the companion volume to the 1996 eight-part PBS series hosted by Hewitt, *Searching for God in America.* Hewitt has won three Emmys for his work on PBS Los Angeles-affiliate KCET's nightly news and public affairs program *Life and Times Tonight,* which Hewitt coanchored for a decade. He served nearly six years in the Reagan Administration in a variety of posts, including the White House counsel's office, and worked with Richard Nixon during Nixon's retirement. Hewitt is a columnist for WorldNetDaily.com.

His Web site is www.HughHewitt.com.

July 2003
Dan + MJ